SET FOR

— THE —

DEFENSE

KENNETH W. GILMORE, SR.

To
Kendric
May God Bless
you in the defense
of your faith!!

Keith Shue

DEDICATION

*This book is dedicated to my good friend and
partner in ministry, John Davis Marshall. I thank
you for your intellectual stimulation, and your
ability to clearly set for your case in defense of the
Christian faith. May God continue to increase
your influence and ministry in our secular culture.*

ACKNOWLEDGMENTS

S*ET FOR THE DEFENSE* WAS DEVELOPED FROM A SEMINAR I
conducted for the Nassau Street Church of Christ in
Tampa, Florida where my good friend Andrew
Atkinson serves as the Minister. As a professor, I have
taught about different aspects of apologetics, but through
this seminar I developed the themes and theses which we
confront in this book.

"Set for the Defense" owes its intellectual development
to so many Christians writers, such as Josh McDowell,
Norman Geisler, Ravi Zachrias, and my two favorite
authors, William Lane Craig and R.C. Sproul. They all
write and teach in such a way that the average believer can
follow technical arguments and speak confidently with the
certainty of his faith.

The Apostle Peter in 1 Peter 3:15 said, "Be ready to give
a defense [answer] for the hope that is within you." **We
must be set for the defense!**

PREFACE

How does a believer answer the scornful skeptics' questions about the validity of the Christian faith? How does the believer present absolute truth in a post-modern society? How does the young, unsuspecting student who enters college withstand the pervasive attacks of godless professors who attempt to destroy their belief system? How does a believer discern various belief systems and world views that are so prevalent in a humanistic society?

In this book I attempt to answer the fundamental objections raised by critics, skeptics, agnostics, and, yes, even atheists: Does God really exist? Is atheism rational? Is the Bible the Word of God? Are miracles possible? Is Jesus really God, and did Jesus rise from the dead?

We can have solid evidence and reasons for our faith. Read and be challenged!

TABLE OF CONTENTS

Acknowledgments vii

Preface ix

Chapter One   Developing A Christian Philosophy . . 1

Chapter Two   What is Apologetics? 17

Chapter Three   Why An Atheist Cannot
                   Be an Atheist 27

Chapter Four   Why I Believe in the Existence
                   of God. 33

Chapter Five   Why I Believe the Bible is the
                   Word of God 45

Chapter Six   Why I Believe that Jesus is God 73

Chapter Seven   Why I Believe in the Resurrection . . 79

Chapter Eight   Why I Believe in Miracles 85

Chapter Nine   God Has Not Left Himself Without a
                   Witness. 89

Chapter Ten   Come Let us Reason. 95

Chapter Eleven   Belief Systems. 103

Chapter Twelve   Apologetic Preaching. 113

Further Reading

Appendix 1   Ten Commandments of
              Apologetics. 119

Appendix 2   Principles of Apologetics 123

Appendix 3   The Unique ness of the Christian
              Message. 125

Appendix 4   Glossary 127

Chapter One

DEVELOPING A CHRISTIAN PHILOSOPHY

FOR MANY BELIEVERS THE WORD "PHILOSOPHY" IS A BUZZ word for heretical or false teachings. This is largely due to the episode found in Acts 17:16-34, where the apostle Paul went to Athens, Greece, known as the intellectual center of the ancient world, to relate Christianity to Greek philosophy. Paul was disturbed when he saw that the city-state of Athens was given over to idols.

In his defense of the Christian faith, Paul stood before the leading thinkers of his day, the Stoics and Epicureans philosophers who "spent their time in nothing else but either to tell or to hear some new thing (v.21)." Paul proclaimed that the God who made the universe does not dwell in temples made with men's hands. And he said that this same God whom these philosophers ignorantly worship a statue with an inscription " to the unknown god," has revealed Himself in the personality of Jesus Christ who, as the God-man, will judge the world by Him.

Second, Paul wrote his letter to the Colossian believers warning them against Gnosticism, to "beware lest anyone cheat you through philosophy and empty deceit, according to the traditions of men, according to the basic principles of this world, and not according to Christ" (Colossians 2:18). It was a warning to avoid philosophy and philosophical discussions.

THE PURPOSE OF PHILOSOPHY

Paul rightly set forth his defense of the Christian faith. Notice that he presented his case for Christ in a logical and systematic way in which the Athenians could understand the truth of his message. But Paul was labeled a babbler (literally translated as the "sperma-logos," which means "seed words").

So the church should challenge and critique philosophies that are adverse to biblical teaching. But philosophy, as a discipline of teaching how to think and make logical or reasonable arguments, will aid us in our preaching and teaching unbelievers about Christ. Taking the passages cited above as examples of avoiding philosophy as a discipline has placed believers in the position of making arguments and positions that are logically flawed. The role of philosophy, or philosophical thinking, is to help us think clearly, precisely, and logically about the basic questions of life: What is reality? What is the nature of reality around us? What is a human being? What happens after death? Is it possible to know anything? How do we know right and wrong? And what is the meaning of human history?

DEVELOPING A CHRISTIAN PHILOSOPHY

The role of philosophy, or philosophical thinking, is to help us think clearly, precisely, and logically about the basic questions of life.

The Bible—and only the Bible—answers these fundamental questions with a degree of finality. As a believer, you are obligated to develop a reasonable perspective of philosophy, a Christian philosophy to answer these questions. This requires the ability to think and reason by using your mind for the task of bringing people to Christ.

Throughout the Scriptures, God challenges His people to use their minds. The battle for the lives of men will be won in the battle of ideas. This is why it so important for believers to know how to think clearly, logically, and consistently to engage a contemporary mindset that has been largely shaped by philosophers from Greece, Europe, and America. Many of these ideas that are prevalent today are not new; they have been circulating for centuries.

Thinking is integral for our call as believers to be what God wants us to be. God calls every believer to think—and to think as well as we can. Jesus says in Luke 10:27: "We are to love God with our mind as well as with our heart, soul, and strength."

Thinking is also integral to our ability to act righteously. Truth and spirituality are part of the same fabric: to know the truth is to do the truth (John 8:31-31). There is no dichotomy between truth (doctrine) and duty (behavior). To be spiritual is to know and to live the truth. Paul says in Romans 12: 1-2 that we should be transformed by the renewing of our minds.

Thinking is also integral to our ability to act righteously.

2 Corinthians 10:3-5 says: "We are to cast down arguments and every high thing that exalts itself against the knowledge of God, bringing every thought into captivity to the obedience of Christ." So God's way to the heart (devotion) is through the head (intellect). So what is philosophy?

DEFINITION

The word "philosophy" comes from two Greek words: "philo," which means "to love," and "Sophia," which means "wisdom." So philosophy in its simplest definition means a lover of wisdom. In ancient Greece, the early philosophers were called "naturalist philosophers," such as Thales, Heraclitus, and Pythagoras, who lived during the 6th century B.C. The naturalist philosophers laid the foundation for Western scientific and philosophical inquiry of keen observation, systematic analysis, and reasons (the laws of inductive and deductive reasoning).

The naturalist philosophers were cosmologists. They believed the world contained order, beauty, regularity, and that the world was rational. Naturalists believed that events in the world could be explained in natural causes (the law of causality—the law of cause and effect—for every effect there must be a cause). These early philosophers were also materialists who believed that the world or universe consists of matter or substance.

SOCRATES

When Socrates (470-399 B.C.) appeared on the scene, philosophy had taken a serious shift from its focus on natural or physical sciences (concentration on the universe) to focusing on the ethical behavior of man. Socrates developed the "Socratic method" or the "dialectical method." Socrates would question the ethical, moral, and political choices of people. His objective was to get people to think and ask why do they make the choices they make? The question of right conduct was central to his life and teachings. Socrates argued that the unexamined life is not worth living. He challenged his peers on matters of public and private virtue, constantly posing the question, what is the greatest good?

Socrates was committed to free inquiry, the freedom to ask why, and not to just go along with the status quo because everybody else accepts something to be true. He would say, listen to your conscience, the inner man, as to what is true. If you don't know something, keep asking questions of yourself and others until you find out. Socrates believed in free thinking.

PLATO

Plato (428-347 B.C.) was a student of Socrates, He established the Academy in Athens, considered the first university in Europe. Plato believed that men had to use their own brains to reach conclusions based upon observation and reason. Plato argued that there is an eternal world of ideas (prototype). We do not experience reality in the so-called "real world," only its dim shadow. This makes sense when you look at the wording of the apostle Paul in 2 Corinthians 4:18: "While we do not look at the things which are seen, but at things which are not seen. For the things which are seen are temporary, but the things which are not seen are eternal."

Plato believed in the eternal world of ideas, that is, the ideal reality is perfect, immutable, or changeless. And the visible objects we see around us are inferior, and they change. If something is perfect, it does not need to change. Heavenly bodies change (the moon, the stars, sun): their change is constant and regular. And this could not happen by chance, but they presuppose a moving soul, endowed with a mind. So Plato reasoned there must be a divine mind that moves the heavens.

Plato believed in a transcendent world of being, and a space-time world of becoming.

ARISTOTLE

Aristotle (384-322 B.C.) was a teacher of Alexander the Great and a student of Plato. Aristotle's name is often associated with the idea of logic. Aristotle did not invent logic; he simply defined what logic is and set forth its fundamental components. Aristotle knew that logic was a supreme tool necessary for all other disciplines of study. Logic is paramount to any intellectual discourse, because that which is unintelligible is not only misunderstood, but it is incapable of being understood. The purpose of logic is to measure or analyze the relationship or statements or prepositions. It can show that conclusions of syllogism are valid or invalid; it does not defend the truth of a conclusion or argument. Arguments are not true and neither are they

> Arguments are not true and neither are they false, but the logical relationship of one statement to another is either valid or invalid.

false, but the logical relationship of one statement to another is either valid or invalid.

Aristotle wrote about the fundamental laws of logic, including "the law of non-contradictions," in which something cannot be what it is and not be what it is not at the same time and in the same sense or relationship. For example, I am an African-American male; I cannot be a Chinese male, or a Hispanic male at the same time. A woman is a woman. We cannot say that she is a woman and a man at the same time. She may be a mother, wife, daughter—but she is still a woman.

Aristotle also presented four distinct types of causes which had been discovered earlier by the naturalistic philosophers in the 6th century B.C. But Aristotle categorized these four types of causes which produce changes: 1) the formal cause which defines what something is; 2) the material cause out of which something is made; 3) the efficient cause by which something is made; and 4) the final cause for which something is made or has purpose.

The dynamics of change concern the ideas of potentiality and actuality. The ultimate cause of motion, which produces change, is rooted in the idea of a pure being or pure actuality. This pure being must be eternal, immutable, and immaterial. Aristotle called this pure being, which is eternal, immutable (not physical), and immutable (doesn't change), the unmoved mover or the uncaused cause. This uncaused cause or unmoved mover for the believer is none other than God Himself.

THE VALUE OF PHILOSOPHY

Philosophy primarily concerns your ability to think logically and consistently about how you make sense of the world. Go into any social situation and hear people discussing the various issues of life—politics, religion, sex, racial issues, justice, education, parenting, marriage, and death. Everybody will share his perspective or philosophy of life on these and many other issues.

But for believers, the benefits of developing a Christian philosophy will equip them to give a reason for believing in God and the defense of historical and biblical Christianity. But how do we philosophize? The three ways we have of thinking are known as "speculative," "analyze," and "prescription."

SPECULATE

Speculative philosophy describes the kind of thinking we do when we are trying to understand the meaning of something.

ANALYZE

Analytical philosophy concerns the idea of breaking things down into parts and examining the relationship between and among those parts.

PRESCRIPTION

Prescriptive philosophy deals with value judgments that we make concerning things in our lives whether they are good or bad.

THREE BRANCHES OF PHILOSOPHY

The three branches in the discipline of philosophy are called "metaphysics," "epistemology," and "axiology."

The three branches in the discipline of philosophy are called "metaphysics," "epistemology," and "axiology."

METAPHYSICAL PHILOSOPHY

The word "metaphysical" comes from two Greek words: "meta," which means "beyond," and "physics," which means "discernible." Metaphysical philosophy deals with the "speculative way of doing philosophy. Metaphysical philosophy is concerned with the study of being or reality. What is reality? Is it natural or supernatural, temporal or eternal, material or immaterial?

EPISTEMOLOGY PHILOSOPHY

Epistemology comes from two Greek words: "episteme," which means "to know," and "logos," which means "to study." So epistemology is the study of knowledge. It deals with question, how do we know anything? Do we acquire knowledge through reason, intuition, traditions, religion, empiricism, agnosticism, and idealism?

Epistemology considers whether ideas are innate or whether we are born a *tabula rasa,* that is, with a blank slate or mind. It deals further with the tests for truth and whether ideas are coherent or need an ultimate foundation or self-evident principles. Epistemology deals with the certainty and doubt.

AXIOLOGY PHILOSOPHY

Axiology philosophy deals with the study of values in ethics and aesthetics. This deals with making value judgments or statements. The subject of ethics involves the issues of moral behavior—both public and private virtues.

AESTHETICS PHILOSOPHY

Aesthetic philosophy is the formal study of "beauty": what is it and what features or characteristics make something "beautiful" in our eyes.

FIDEISM

When we, as believers, have discussions with agnostics and atheists, our tendency is to try to hold a dialogue about the Bible. Unbelievers do not accept our beginning premise that the Bible is the Word of God. They do not believe in God, therefore the Bible has no validity to them as a criteria for determining what is truth and what is not truth.

As believers, we argue that the validity of the Christian faith should not rest upon rational or philosophical arguments outside the Bible. Our position has been that the truth of the Christian faith rests entirely on our faith and not on reasonable evidence outside the Bible; in other words, religious belief is not supported by reason.

They do not believe in God, therefore the Bible has no validity to them as a criteria for determining what is truth and what is not truth.

The emphasis on the operation of faith to ascertain the truth claims of the Christian faith is called "fideism" by philosophers. Fideism, as a methodology for establishing the truth of the Christian world view, is completely inadequate. Remember, epistemology deals with how do we know anything? The believer is right when he says there is a God, but how can he prove this assertion outside the confines of the Bible? How do you know the Bible is the Word of God? Why not the Koran or other holy Scriptures? Agnostics and atheists would argue that your faith is in your faith, which is a leap in the darkness.

Philosophy helps us to advance the case that Christianity is the most logical and consistent belief, given all the facts, than any other world view. So the believer does not have to be afraid of using philosophy to frame carefully crafted and organized positions on the validity of the Christian faith.

We need to use the intellectual resources we have at our disposal to proclaim the source of our faith.

The church is called upon in every age to present a coherent account of its faith and to testify to that living truth with which it has been entrusted—the gospel of Christ. The church's articulation and proclamation cannot be limited to one intellectual approach of dogmatism. We need to use the intellectual resources we have at our disposal to proclaim the source of our faith.

The task of thinking responsibly about God and about faith is the essence of the church's mission. Faith is generally seen by the larger society as a hindrance rather than an asset. Bringing explicit faith commitments into the public domain is inappropriate precisely because the truths of Christianity are not and can never be demonstrable.

Trevor Hart, in his book *Faith Thinking: The Dynamics of Christian Theology* (1995), says that society forces Christians to live in two different worlds. We have dual passports, allowing us to pass freely from the world of our private commitments into the world of public intercourse and back again with no questions asked. The only demand is that we at all times must remember which world we are in. Because the rules by which conduct is governed in each world are quite different. Hart further contends that this kind of compartmentalizing of our lives encourages Christianity to be hung up in the wardrobe with our Sunday best or left on the bedside table together with our Bibles, rather than being carried with us into the office, the factory, or wherever, as salt and light for a society in need of purification and illumination.

To keep quiet about faith is simply wrong. Christ calls us to share it, lay it before others for their consideration, and to allow it to shape and mold our thinking and action in every sphere of life. It is to this end that we now turn to deal with the issue of apologetics—giving a reasonable defense for the faith we have!

STUDY QUESTIONS

1. Define the word "philosophy."
2. What does the author say is the purpose of philosophy?
3. What reasons does the author give for why some Christians do not like philosophy?
4. Who was Plato and what was his contribution to philosophy?
5. Who was Socrates and what was his contribution to philosophy?
6. Who was Aristotle and what was his contribution to philosophy?
7. What are the three branches of philosophy?
8. What is epistemology?
9. Define the word "fideism."

Chapter Two

WHAT IS APOLOGETICS?

THE OBJECTIVE OF EVANGELISM IS TO WIN THE WORLD TO Christ by the preaching of the Gospel by "warning and teaching every man to present them perfect in Christ" (Colossians 1:28). Apologetics deals with the defense of the Christian faith by giving reasonable and intelligent answers to those questions to which skeptics and atheists raise in their objection to Christianity as being valid and trustworthy.

DEFINITION OF APOLOGETICS

The term "apologetics" comes from the Greek word apologia, apo, meaning "from," and logia from logos, meaning "word," "thought," "speech," or "reason." So apologia means from a word, thought or reason. The word was often used in arguments given in a court of law. The word also had the idea of judicial interrogation where a person is called to answer for the manner in which he has exercised his responsibility as a citizen.

"Apologetics" also means a formal explanation or defense of a position (1 Corinthians 9:3; 2 Corinthians 7:11). The word would also apply in giving answers to the skeptical, abusive, and sarcastic critics who ridicule the Christian faith.

The fundamental problem with nonbelievers is not their intellectual objections but their morality. In Ephesians 2:1ff, Paul said that the unsaved person is dead in sin. As we share the Gospel, we must realize that the people to whom we are trying to communicate are spiritually dead, and the Holy Spirit must do the quickening to bring to life. The Holy Spirit does this by taking the Gospel message and applying it to the heart (mind) of the nonbeliever.

The fundamental problem with nonbelievers is not their intellectual objections but their morality.

FOUR CATEGORIES OF PEOPLE

JUDAISM

There are many people who believe in God, yet they reject Jesus Christ as God. Orthodox Jews believe in the God (Yahweh) of the Old Testament (Torah), yet they reject Jesus as God's chosen one—the Messiah (Christ-Anointed One). Jesus said in John 12:48, "He that rejects me and receives not my words has one to judge him in the last days, the words that I have spoken shall judge him in the last days."

ISLAM

Islam is dedicated to the fundamental question of who God is. Islam is committed to the idea of the unity and singularity of God (Surah 4:116). Islam does not reject the God of the Old Testament, but it does reject His name, as recorded in the Old Testament. Islam contends that God's name is not Yahweh but Allah. Islam teaches Jesus was the Messiah (Surah 5:14:25). Islam further contends that Jesus was a great prophet in succession of other great prophets, but God's final prophet, Muhammad, is the seal of all the prophets (Surah 19:29-31; 5:110).

The Koran (holy book for Islam) is believed by Muslims to be verbally inspired and dictated by the angel Gabriel to Muhammad from the eternal copy in heaven. Muslims further believe that the Koran and the hadith (Muslim traditions) are the two essential books. We will discover that 60 percent of the Koran consists of misconstrued stories from the Bible. The problem with the Koran is that it contains many biblical stories that are taken out of chronological order. The Koran teaches the virgin birth of Christ as a supernatural event, that Jesus performed many miracles (Surah 19:19-21; 3:7-47), and that God raised Jesus from the dead (Surah 4:158).

The Koran further teaches that Jesus was a prophet, and that all the prophets were sinless (Surah 28:16). So if all the prophets were sinless and Jesus was a prophet and lying is a sin, how can the Koran dismiss what Jesus said about Himself? Jesus clearly taught that He was God manifest in flesh. Jesus claimed He had the power to forgive sins. No one could forgive sins except God alone. Jesus said that "when you see me you see the Father" (John 14:6-7). Jesus is the only prophet who 1) had a supernatural birth and life, 2) performed miracles, and 3) ascended in heaven, which was never said of any other prophets.

UNITARIANS

Unitarians also believe in one God, monotheism. The word Mono-one, Theism-God. Biblical Christianity also teaches there is one God. But within monotheism are three person-alities, Father, Son, and the Holy Spirit, which comprises the Godhead. Unitarians reject the idea of the Trinity-Trithree- unity-one, in spite of what Jesus taught that He was co-equal, co-eternal, co-essence with the Father.

There is no difference between the Father, Son, and the Holy Spirit. Christ is eternal, He always existed, and there never was a time when He did not exist.

JEHOVAH WITNESSES

Jehovah Witnesses teach a belief about Christ that originated in the second century known as Aryanism. Aryanism denied the deity of Christ and taught that He was a created being. Closely associated with Aryanism was Gnosticism, which comes from the Greek word "gnosis," which means to know. Gnosticism denied the humanity of Christ. The Gnostics believed that God is Holy, and if He is indeed holy, why would He contaminate himself with matter that is evil in the incarnation (virgin birth). So John the apostle explained in all his letters that Jesus was incarnated in human flesh. "Docetism" teaches that Jesus had only the appearance of being human. All cults attack the validity of the deity of Christ.

THERE ARE TWO TYPES OF PEOPLE

Nonbelievers are comprised of agnostics, atheists, secular humanists (who teach that man is the measure of all things), and those who follow pragmatism. So when we talk to people about the validity of the Christian faith, we need to understand where nonbelievers are coming from. Religious believers are comprised of Jews, Muslims, Jehovah Witnesses, Mormons, polytheists, Hindus, New Age Religionists, and Christians—those who have embraced historical biblical Christianity.

Each of these belief systems embraces a reality that cancels out the other. All these beliefs claim they have the truth, but all these beliefs cannot be right. The idea that all religions lead to God is a false premise that is based on the philosophy of religious pluralism and tolerance. Many people are religious today, but because they are religious does not make them Christians.

The Bible claims that it is absolute truth. Western culture teaches there are no absolute truths, but everything is relative. Truths are facts which correspond to reality. When a person says there is no absolute truth, that statement itself becomes an absolute statement. In order for their statement to be true, the statement itself must be an absolute truth.

WHAT IS PROOF?

There are nonbelievers who say, prove to me that the Bible is the Word of God. Prove to me that God exists. There are four types of proof the believer can appeal to in establishing the truth of the Christian faith.

HISTORICAL PROOF

People living today have never seen George Washington, the first president of the United States. But because they have never seen him does not dismiss the historical fact that George Washington existed. We know he existed based upon historical documents (birth certificate, letters, newspapers, pictures, eyewitness accounts, artifacts (personal items, such as shoes, clothes, rings, watches, and so forth).

Historical proof can aid us in the verification of truth. When it comes to the New Testament, the skeptic will say, how do we know that Jesus ever existed? There is historical proof that Jesus existed outside the pages of the New Testament.

Extra biblical sources include ancient historians such as Tactius, Suetonius, and Thallus. Jewish sources: Josephus. The Jewish Talmud, Government officials: Pliny, the younger, Trajan, the Roman Emperor, Hadrian, the Roman emperor, and Gnostic gospels. Overall, at least 17 non-Christian sources record more than 50 details concerning Jesus. These sources date back 20 to 150 years after Jesus's death. These secular sources are quite early by the standards of ancient historians.

Meteorologists can predict weather patterns based upon observation and analysis. No evidence is 100 percent certain. The only way that evidence is 100 percent certain is when we are there to see the person or event. (Most historical evidence is beyond the time frame in which we live, and we have to rely upon someone else's testimony.)

SCIENTIFIC PROOF

Scientific truth operates off the principle of observation, reason, analysis, repeatable events, and hypothesis.

Scientific truth operates off the principle of observation, reason, analysis, repeatable events, and hypothesis. Scientific proof says in order for something to be true, we have to see it (observe it), and it must be repeatable (observations that can be repeated). It is analyzed and then scientists make a hypothesis or general theory of how something will work.

For example, the sun comes up in the east and will always set in the west. How can scientists make this statement? Because it has been observed through the natural physical eyes. It has been continually repeated, and then hypothesized as to the cycle of the sun rising and setting.

LEGAL PROOF

In our judicial system we have what is called the "preponderance of evidence." The phrase "preponderance of evidence" says all the evidence points to the accused, and it is impossible for the state to rule the accused out as a suspect who committed the crime. Preponderance is the weight of the evidence. It could be pictures, documents, eyewitness testimony, circumstantial evidence, finger prints or DNA samples.

MANY PEOPLE REJECT CHRISTIANITY BASED ON TWO REASONS

THE PROBLEM OF EVIL

Many nonbelievers are angry at God for some tragic event that has befallen them. The loss of a loved one, such as in the terrorist attack on the World Trade Center. They raised the crucial question, why would God allow such horrific evil to happen on that tragic day, September 11, 2001. Why would God allow 6 million Jews to be exterminated in Hitler's gas chambers? Why would God permit slaves to be treated with such physical abuse during the days of slavery. Why would Got permit segregation and Jim Crowism? Why would God allow innocent children to suffer and die in African nations and other countries around the world?

WILLFUL UNBELIEF

Many nonbelievers have made up their minds that they will never become Christians. They have made a conscious choice to live a life of unbelief. John 3:17 says: "He who does not believe in Christ is judged already because he will not believe in the name of the only Son of God. This is the judgment that light has come in the world and men love darkness rather than light because their deeds were evil."

In Romans 1:18-22: "For the wrath of God is revealed from Heaven against all ungodliness and unrighteousness of men, who suppress (hold down) the truth in unrighteousness, because what may be known of God is manifest in them, for God has shown it to them. For clearly seen, being understood by the things that are made, even His eternal power and Godhead so that they are without excuse, because, although they know God, they did not glorify Him as God, nor were thankful but became futile in their thoughts, and their foolish hearts were darkened. Professing to be wise, they became fools. . . ."

STUDY QUESTIONS

1. What does the term "apologetic" mean?
2. What is the fundamental problem with unbelievers?
3. What are the four categories people fall into?
4. What are the two types of people in the world?
5. How many types of proof does the author give for rejecting Christianity?

Chapter Three

WHY AN ATHEIST CANNOT BE AN ATHEIST

Romans 1:17ff: "For the wrath of God is revealed from heaven against all ungodliness and unrighteousness of men who hold the truth in unrighteousness."

The atheist knows the truth but refuses to believe the truth. As a matter fact, they suppress the truth to keep the truth from being revealed. The apostle writing to the Romans explained that the atheist is without excuse because God has revealed Himself in three specific ways: Creation, Conscience, and Christ.

CREATION

"Because that which is known by God is manifest in them for God has shown it unto them. Since the creation of the world, His invisible attributes, His eternal power and divine nature have been clearly seen in the things that have been made, so that they are without excuse."

God has revealed himself in creation. This is called "natural law" or "natural revelation." The nonbeliever can behold nature and discover in nature that there is a creator who exists. This is called a "self-evident truth."

> The Bible makes no attempt to prove the existence of God.

The Bible makes no attempt to prove the existence of God. It states the existence of God as a self-evident truth. This is why the Psalmist in Psalm 14 says, *"The fool has said in his heart there is no God."*

All the nonbeliever has to do is ask the question, why am I here? How did I get here? How do I explain the miracle of birth? There is something mysterious about human existence.

CONSCIENCE OF MAN

Man differs from the animals in that he can observe, think, and arrive at logical conclusions. He is endowed by God, his creator, with understanding. In the New Testament, this is called his "mind" or "heart"; it is the intellectual principle that God gave to man when He created him. As a result of the fall, his mind has become darkened. Theologians like to refer to this as the "noetic effects of sin." The word "noetic" derives form the Greek word for "mind," which is "nous."

Originally, man's mind could absorb and analyze information much better and more accurately than he can now. He could understand truth correctly without distortion. His mind is now clouded by sin. After the fall, man still possesses a mind. He can still think. He can still reason. He has not lost the faculty of the mind but the facility is lost. What was once easy is now difficult. His reason has been clearly affected by sin in his fallen state.

In Romans 1:28, Paul said: "And even they [men] did not like to retain God in their knowledge. God gave them over to a reprobate [rejected, worthy of condemnation, useless, evil] mind." But even in man's fall state, God has not left Himself without a witness. In Acts 14:16-17, Luke recorded the words of Paul when he said, "Who in bygone generations allowed all nations to walk in their own ways. Nevertheless He did not leave Himself without witness, in that He did good, gave us rain from heaven and fruitful seasons, filling our hearts with food and gladness."

In Romans 2:14-16, Paul said again, "For when Gentiles, who do not have the law, by nature do the things in the law, these although do not have the law, are a law to themselves, who show the work of the law written in their hearts [mind], their conscience also bearing witness, and between themselves their thoughts accusing or else excusing them in that day when God will judge the secrets of men by Jesus Christ, according to my gospel."

So not only has God revealed Himself in creation, in the conscience of men, but also in the personality of Christ [we will deal with the uniqueness of Christ in Chapter Four].

IS ATHEISM RATIONAL?

An atheist says he knows God does not exist. If he claims he knows that God does not exist, this statement is a self-contradiction. To say God does not exist is to say first of all that the atheist knows all things. Second, the atheist's statement declares he is present everywhere at one time. And third, the atheist's statement indicates that he is all powerful.

When the atheist claims he knows God does not exist, he is claiming he knows all reality—he knows all truth.

When the atheist claims he knows God does not exist, he is claiming he knows all reality—he knows all truth. And we know this is not true. But to make the statement that God does not exist is an absolute statement. And the question is, if we do not know all things, is it possible that God may exist in what we do not know?

If the atheist does not know everything, then God may exist in what he does not know. If the atheist himself is not all powerful and cannot be everywhere at one time, it is possible that God may be somewhere that he is not at that time. Is it possible that God may be playing hiding and seek with him?

> If the atheist does not know everything, then God may exist in what he does not know.

To make the claim that God does not exist is to say we know all things, we are all powerful and we are everywhere at one time. If the atheist possesses any of these attributes, he would be God because these are the attributes which are ascribed to God himself—that He is all knowing, all powerful, and is everywhere at one time (omnipotent—all powerful, omniscience—all knowing, omnipresent—all present).

Atheism is a relatively new belief system. It was not until the Age of the Enlightenment in the seventeenth century when people began to question the idea of the existence of God. This was the belief of eighteenth century Scottish philosopher David Hume. Prior to this in Western Civilization people believed in the supernatural. But with the rise of science, people began to question the existence of God.

AGNOSTICISM

The atheist is really not an atheist; he is an agnostic. An agnostic says there is not enough information to believe or disbelieve, therefore he will suspend all judgment in regard to the question of the existence of God.

But the agnostic cannot really be an agnostic because there are sufficient reasons to believe in the existence of God. It is to these reasons we turn to in the next chapter.

STUDY QUESTIONS

1. What three specific ways has God revealed Himself to mankind?
2. What is an atheist?
3. What is an agnostic?
4. What three reasons does the author give for why atheism is irrational?

Chapter Four

WHY I BELIEVE IN THE EXISTENCE OF GOD

HRISTIANS DID NOT THROW AWAY THEIR BRAINS WHEN they accepted Jesus as their personal Savior. There are intellectual reasons why Christians believe in the existence of God. The traditional arguments for the existence of God was developed by the late Medieval theologian Thomas Aquinas. Thomas Aquinas described the arguments as "reasons" for the existence of God.

THE COSMOLOGICAL ARGUMENT (MOTION AND CHANGE)

The word "cosmos" comes from the Greek word kosmos, which is the derivation of the word "cosmetics," which means "to give order." A woman tries to improve her appearance cosmetically—to give order. When we talk about the cosmos, we are talking about the universe which has order and design.

The cosmological argument deals with the idea that in the universe change and motion are taking place. If we look through a telescope, we will notice that the celestial bodies (the moon, stars, planets) are in a constant state of change.

The universe is not static. It is not standing still, but it is dynamic and moving. If the universe is in motion and not static, how do we explain motion? Everything that moves is moved by something. If we go to a lake and throw a stone, we will discover a rippling effect that has been caused as a result of the stone. The rippling effect of the water has its origin when the stone is thrown into the lake.

So it is with the universe. It is in motion because something is moving it. For motion must have a cause. Ancient Greek philosopher Aristotle said this is happening because of the "unmoved mover" or the "uncaused cause." Aristotle believed in a Supreme Being but would not ascribe this Supreme Being with the God of the Bible.

Since the universe is in state of motion; it is not eternal because something that is eternal never changes. And since the universe is in a state of motion and change, then there must be a cause and effect in the world. One event (the effect) is explained by the influence of another (the cause). This principle is called the law of causality. This principle states that for every effect there must be a cause.

The big bang theory would arise out of the cosmological argument. Theologians have argued if there was in fact a big bang, what caused the bang? Something had to begin the big bang.

Albert Einstein formulated the theory of relativity in 1905. This theory conceded time had begun somewhere back in eternity. The idea of motion is traced back to a single cause. God is the single cause.

ONTOLOGICAL ARGUMENT (EXISTENCE OF CONTINGENT BEING)

The ontological argument deals with contingent and non-contingent beings. For example, a rock is a non-being, but all living creatures, such as plants, animals—and man, are living beings.

A plant is a higher form of life than a rock because a rock is a non-being. An animal is higher form of life than plants because plants do not have instinct and emotions. What makes man different? Man is a higher form of being than animals because animals do not have a personality, a will, an intellect, and emotions as humans do. So if man is a higher form of being, then there must be a being which is a higher form of being than man. We would called that being God because God has a will, intellect, and emotions.

CONTINGENT BEINGS

The fact that we are here and exist needs some explanation as to why we exist. Why are all of these beings different?

The fact that we are here and exist needs some explanation as to why we exist.

The world contains beings (such as ourselves), and we are not here by necessity. Necessity means our existence here on this planet is necessary in order for this planet to exist. If this were true, then we would not die. We are here by the will of our parents.

NON-CONTINGENT BEINGS

Let us contrast a type of being who is here as a matter of necessity. God is a necessary being and we are contingent beings. Why? Because God is transcendent; He is all powerful; He knows all things, and He is everywhere at the same time. He exists in and of himself and all by himself. He does not need us; we need him. "In him we live and move and have our very existence." We depend on God.

A non-necessary or contingent being is here or comes into existence because something which already existed brought it into being. Man is brought here because God created him into existence (Genesis 1:26-27). Man's existence is caused by another (God).

EVOLUTION AND THE BIBLE

In 1859, Charles Darwin's theory of evolution by natural selection appeared in his book titled *On the Origin of Species*. There are two types of evolution. There is macro evolution and there is micro evolution.

MACRO EVOLUTION

Macro evolution says there are changes and adaptations within species to adapt to their environment in which they live. Built inside of these species' DNA system is the ability to adapt to their environment. Natural selection allows organisms to do what God commanded them to do—to be fruitful and multiply.

For example, a polar bear can adapt to the nature of his environment in a cold climate, but a grizzly bear could not adapt to a much colder climate in Alaska because nature has not fitted him for such an environment.

But there are certain species that can survive and adapt to different climates and environment. So there are changes within species that allow them to change according to their environments.

MICRO EVOLUTION

Micro evolution says there are significant changes within a species. That species can change into another species. For example, a rabbit can change its DNA (the genetic pre-programmed code) to where it can become a dog. The problem with this theory is that it has never happened. Scientists have never proven that such an adaptation and change have ever occurred in any species.

Evolution is a faith system and not a fact system. It also takes faith to believe as well as the Christian faith.

Genesis 1:11: "Every seed produces after its own kind." A plant seed (orange) will produce only an orange. In the animal kingdom, horses produce horses, pigs produce pigs, but never will you find a horse reproducing a pig. Humans reproduce after their own kind. Micro evolution is called "random selection." Evolution is a faith system and not a fact system. It also takes faith to believe as well as the Christian faith.

The problem with evolution is that it is a theory which proposes a formula that is much more difficult to believe than accepting the biblical cosmology about the origin of the universe. Evolution's theoretical formula is based on "nobody times nobody equals everything."

Evolution is degrading to the human family for several reasons because the theory includes the following premises: first, that human life is an accident with no purpose;

second, since we were not created for a purpose, we need not strive to do our best; third, since the human family is a product of evolution, we are no better than the animals. This is why so many people have adopted the philosophy of narcissism (philosophy of self-infatuation or excessive admiration of yourself) and hedonism (philosophy of pleasure to the exclusion of pain).

MORAL ARGUMENTS

Most humans have a sense of moral obligations or sense of right and wrong. This deals with the fact of absolute truth. Anthropologists (those who study man's physical, social, and cultural development and behavior) have discovered in every culture and civilization a set of moral codes which govern conduct in that tribe or culture. Every civilization has a moral code to determine what is right or wrong. These moral codes of conduct may differ from society and cultures and even conflict with each other, but they all have some type of moral code system based on that culture.

If this is true, where did the sense of "morality," "right," and "wrong" come from? Where do values of truth, goodness, and justice come from? Take two little kids in a nursery and give them both a toy. One of the kids sooner or later will take away the toy from the other child who starts to cry. Why does he cry? Because he has experienced unfairness. Where does this moral code of right and wrong come from?

In Romans 2:15, Paul said, "God has revealed in their conscience also bearing witness, and between themselves their thoughts accusing or else excusing them...." Most people have a moral sense of obligation between right and wrong. Morality is not based upon society and instinct. A person's sense of morality might change, but morality itself will never change. There is a moral code or constraint underlying all civilizations.

THE PHILOSOPHY STUDENT

A philosophy student wrote a paper on the subject of ethics. He argued that there were no absolutes, and everything is relative. Judged by the quality and research of the paper, it was well documented. The paper demonstrated scholarship and should have received an "A." The professor gave the paper an "F" with a note explaining he did not like the cover blue!

The student said, "This is not fair! I should be graded on the content."

The professor said, "Is this your paper that you argue? That there is no objective principles, such as fairness and justice and that everything is relative to one's taste?"

"Yes, yes, that's the one," replied the student.

"Well, then," said the professor, "I do not like blue covers. The grade remains an "F."

The moral of the story is that even though the student

had argued in his paper the validity of non-absolute truth and criteria, he still wanted to be judged based upon a standard or criteria which had a moral basis for his cry of unfairness. The origin of the idea of morality suggests there must be a God.

TELEOLOGICAL ARGUMENT (THE PRINCIPLE OF DESIGN AND PURPOSE)

The term "teleological" comes from the Greek word telos, which means "end" or "purpose." The teleological argument deals with intelligent design and purpose. Everything that exists has a design and purpose.

Everything that exists has a design and purpose.

For example, a chair, car, or house were all created with design and purpose. God has created us with design and purpose for our lives. And God wants us to function according to our design and purpose. In Genesis, God designed man to have dominion over his creation. Things do not design themselves—they are caused and designed by someone or something.

For example, a man goes out into the woods and discovers a garden. This garden is designed with each row having different types of vegetables. The man does not see the gardener, but he knows there must be a gardener because he observes an intelligent design and purpose.

Notice a watch's design. Its purpose is to keep time. We know because of the intricate design and purpose of the watch. Even though we do not see the watchmaker, we know that a watchmaker exists because of the design and purpose of the watch.

ANTHROPIC PRINCIPLE (THE UNIVERSE IS FINELY TUNED)

Science recognizes that the solar system of the universe is a finely tuned system in order for life to exist.

The anthrophic principle states that the Creation account in the book of Genesis gives 10 specific steps of creation that Moses describes. Each of these steps has been embraced as being essential for life to exist on this planet. Science recognizes that the solar system of the universe is a finely tuned system in order for life to exist.

The anthrophic principle points to intelligent design which further points to a creator. The cosmos was designed, rather than by chance, as evolution teaches.

STUDY QUESTIONS

1. What are the five reasons the author gives for the existence of God?
2. What is the Cosmological argument?
3. What is the Ontological argument?
4. What is the Moral argument?
5. What is the Teleological argument?
6. What is the Anthropic argument?
7. What is a contingent being?
8. What is a non-contingent being?
9. What is Macro evolution?
10. What is Micro evolution?

Chapter Five

WHY I BELIEVE THE BIBLE IS THE WORD OF GOD

THE FOLLOWING CLEARLY LAYS OUT THE CASE FOR WHY I believe the Bible is the Word of God.

REVELATION

Revelation is God's supernatural disclosure of His will to man. God makes known what was previously not known to men. It reveals the will of God. When God revealed His will to men, they wrote down what God had communicated to them. This is called "inspiration." These writings became Scripture, the Word of God. Inspiration makes the claim that God's word is infallible.

INSPIRATION

Paul said in 2 Timothy 3:16-17 that "all Scripture is given by the inspiration of God." The word "inspiration" comes from the Greek word Theos- God pnumetos –pneumatic- which means "wind," "breath," or "spirit." So when Paul said all Scripture is given by the inspiration of God—the Scriptures are God-breathed.

Inspiration deals with words that have been God-inspired or God-breathed; they came from the mouth of God.

In Matthew 4:1ff, Jesus was driven out into the wilderness by the Holy Spirit and was tempted 40 days and 40 nights. The tempter came to him and said to him turn these stones into bread. Jesus quoted from Deuteronomy 8:8 that "man shall not live by bread alone, but by every word that proceeds out of the mouth of God." Inspiration deals with words that have been God-inspired or God-breathed; they came from the mouth of God.

INERRANCY

God's word is inerrant—the revelation of God contains no errors or contradiction. Men are finite—limited because they are human. But God is not finite. He is infinite. He has no limits. So the revelation God had given to man shows him the right direction without error. God's word is in fact himself, because His word represents His character and His nature.

Isaiah 55:6: "Seek the Lord while He may be found, call upon Him while He is near, let the wicked forsake His way and the unrighteous man His thoughts and let him return to the Lord and He will give mercy on him; and to our God, for He will abundantly pardon. For my thoughts are not your thoughts, nor are your ways my ways as the Lord. For as the heavens are higher than the earth, so are my ways are higher than your ways and my thoughts your thoughts. So shall my word be that goes forth from my mouth. It shall not return to me word, but it shall accomplish what I please, and it shall prosper in the thing for which I sent it."

When God speaks, He has creative power. He calls things into existence. Romans 4:17: "God calls those things that be not as though they were." Jeremiah 1:12: "The Lord said to me, you have seen well, for I am watching over my word to perform." When God speaks a word, it will come to past. We can rely on the Word of God.

The very survival of the Christian faith depends on the reliability and the authority of the Bible. If the claims of the Bible are not true, if it is found to be false, then the whole Christian faith collapses. If we mistrust the Bible, then the Bible has no valid purpose in our life. If you can discount it, then it has no credibility. One of the major challenges of cults is to destroy the Bible as the Word of God.

The Bible is the testing ground and the litmus test for every cult and religious group to determine whether we are dealing with truth or error. If the Bible can be shown to be incorrect, then the church must cease its business and go on about the daily routine of living with no real significance to life. All truth claims of the Christian faith depend on the Bible for its truthfulness because every religious issue, claim or doctrine must be examined to see if it is true. And we must examine whether we have the authority to teach or practice something. When we follow the Bible, we have the authority of heaven to do it.

> The Bible is the testing ground and the litmus test for every cult and religious group to determine whether we are dealing with truth or error.

Some spiritual truths in the Bible cannot be verified scientifically, historically, or legally. We cannot prove heaven, hell, angels, Holy Spirit, or God. Why? Because the Bible is a faith book. "We walk by faith and not by sight." But this does not mean that because the Bible is a faith book that Christianity is not a logical and unreasonable faith. There are reasons for why Christians believe what they believe.

The Bible can be demonstrated as being truthful and reliable in the areas to be investigated: history, archaeology, culture of the time, and the geographical milieu.

TEXTURAL COHERENCE

A common theme runs from Genesis to Revelation—from the Old Testament to the New Testament. The Bible was written over a period of 1,500 years, and it was written by 40 different authors.

Since it was written more than1,500 years ago by 40 different writers, many of these writers did not know one another; their occupations and vocations were different. Some were shepherds, farmers, kings, prophets, fishermen.

These men came from different locations and different walks of life, yet we would think we would find mistakes, errors, and contradictions. But we find consistency and clarity, which is a miracle all by itself. There are prophecies that were made 1,500 years before the event ever transpired or came about; they occurred exactly when and like they were prophesied to happen.

So the Bible says up front that it is a supernatural book—that it came from God. Inspiration means these men were under the guidance and direction of the Holy Spirit. The Holy Spirit guided them in the selection of the materials they would use in recording the information we have in the Bible.

THE BIBLE IS NOT A HISTORY BOOK

Biblical writers did not give us an exhaustive and comprehensive history of the ancient world. Many of the events and people who lived in the ancient world are not recorded in the Bible.

The Biblical writers selected the information that would be relevant and pertinent to the discussion under consideration.

The Biblical writers selected the information that would be relevant and pertinent to the discussion under consideration. This is not foreign to us; the daily newspaper or news channel does not give us all the information and newsworthy events that occurred during the day. They give us only what they consider vital news the public needs to know about and they tell it in 60-second sound bytes.

The biblical writers were the same way. They were selective in the information they gave us. They wanted to give only the essential information because they had a particular point they were trying to make. (See John 21:25, Luke 1:1-4.)

ACCURACY AND ITS TRANSMISSION DOWN THROUGH AGES

Many people will say, how do we know the Bible was translated accurately? Did Europeans write the Bible? The biblical writers were Semitic people, not European. The Bible is an oriental book, written under oriental skies. It was written in the context of an ancient Near Eastern culture.

WHAT HAPPENED TO THE ORIGINAL AUTOGRAPHS?

When the Bible was first written, these men were under the guidance of inspiration. These first documents were called "autographs." The original autographs no longer exist. As the Church was growing, the autographs, especially the New Testament, became necessary in various geographical locations. These were copies of the Scriptures. So copies upon copies were made of the original autographs.

The men who made copies of the Scriptures were called "scribes." Scribes were very careful in what they wrote because in those days printing was not available. The printing press was not invented until 1450. So people had to rely upon the accuracy of the scribes to provide concise copies of the Scriptures.

ORAL TRADITIONS

Ancient Near Eastern cultures were accustomed to oral traditions. Keep in mind the book published in 1976 titled

Roots by Alex Haley. The story Alex Haley wrote was orally transmitted to him by his grandmother, and this and other stories had been orally communicated to her down through the years. He simply recorded on audio tape and eventually transmitted it to paper.

The autographs of the New Testament were transmitted over a period of time. Scribes took great pain in transmitting what they were copying.

MANUSCRIPTS

How do we know that the copies we possess of the Bible are reliable and accurate? How can we today—living 2,000 years removed from the text—be sure we have the biblical text they wrote?

The copies of the original autographs are called "manuscripts." What is the evidence that we can ascertain whether or not the text of the Bible is that of the original writers? We can date the time in which the documents of the original autographs of the New Testament were written.

We know, for example, that the Book of Galatians was written some time around 48 A.D. It was probably the earliest of the New Testament books written. We know that John wrote the Book of Revelation around the year 96 A.D., which fits the time period when the Emperor Domitian was reigning.

We can attest to the dating of the New Testament from the apostolic fathers. The apostolic fathers were church leaders who lived in the latter part of the first century and beginning of the second century. From the writings of the apostolic fathers we can reproduce the entire New Testament.

This is important because scholars can place the entire New Testament documents within the first 100 years of the early Church. In other words, the entire New Testament was written in the first century and in the lifetime of many of the eyewitnesses who were still living when the New Testament was completed or the canon was closed (Luke 1:1-4).

Some skeptics and critics would say the New Testament came many years after the apostles died. Luke said there were

The entire New Testament was written in the first century and in the lifetime of many of the eyewitnesses who were still living when the New Testament was completed or the canon was closed.

many writers who compiled a narrative of what had transpired and had taken place in the early church. There was already in existence a written body of truth available to the early church.

Luke said that he checked or investigated his sources carefully. As a mater fact, he said the sources he checked were "eyewitnesses" of the events concerning the life of Jesus, His crucifixion and resurrection. Who were these eyewitnesses? They were the apostles themselves. Luke is writing his gospel to an important Roman official by the name of Theophilus so that he may know the certainty of what Christians believe.

We depend today upon eyewitness testimony of people who were alive at such events as the assassination of Martin Luther King, Jr., in 1968. They can testify whether a writer or speaker today may say about those events 35 years later as to the veracity of their statements. Why? Because they were there when it happened.

This is contrary to what liberal scholarship in the last 150 years had been advocating—that the New Testament was written in the second and third century by disciples who wrote these documents in the name of the apostles after they had died.

The duplicity of New Testament scholarship is that oftentimes it will accept the veracity of secular writers over biblical writers when the evidence for biblical writers far surpasses the test of the veracity of historical literature. For example the only manuscript we have of the writings of Plato comes 900 hundred years after Plato lived. The writings of the New Testament appeared 15 to 30 years after Jesus died.

THE NEW TESTAMENT HAS A WIDE GEOGRAPHICAL DISTRIBUTION

The New Testament was not just written to the Church in Jerusalem, Corinth, Ephesus. We find copies of manuscripts from all over the ancient world. All those churches in the ancient world had the same body of truth because all of them taught and held the same beliefs (1 Corinthians 1:1-4; 4:17).

THE NEW TESTAMENT IS THE BEST ATTESTED WORK FROM THE ANCIENT WORLD

We have more than 5,000 partial or complete Greek manuscripts. This is important because there is no other book that has been produced or has come to us from the ancient world that contains more manuscripts than the New Testament.

We have in existence three of the most important manuscripts in our possession today that go back to the fourth century. They are housed in the British Museum in London, the Vatican Library in Rome, and Saint Catherine Monastery at the base of Mount Sinai.

We have the codex Sinaitcus (fourth century in the British Museum), the codex Alexandrinus (British Museum), and the codex Vaticanus (Vatican Library in Rome). These manuscripts possess all the books of the New

Testament. We also have overwhelming evidence of manuscripts that are Syriac and Coptic. This is important because when scholars examine these manuscripts from different cultures, geography, languages, and time periods, not one of these manuscripts contradicts the other.

Textual criticism is the science which determines the original words of the New Testament. It contends that the New Testament is 99.9 percent accurate in its transmission from the autographs and manuscripts to our English translation today.

THE WRITING OF THE NEW TESTAMENT

Behind the New Testament lies a unique story of a book written not only by the hand of men, but by the hand of God: the New Testament speaks with an authority unknown to other books, and which is as up to date as when it was written centuries ago.

The first of the New Testament documents did not appear until 15 to 20 years after the death of Christ. Why the delay? As long as Jesus lived on earth, His followers felt no need for any new written documents. Jesus himself is recorded to have written nothing except what He wrote in the sand in John 8.

A second factor was that even after the Lord's death, His followers expected Him to return soon (1 Corinthians 7:29, 3,1, for example). If the second coming was immediate, there was neither the time nor the reason to write books.

A third reason in the delay in the production of New Testament Scripture was the Palestinian aversion of writing other books in addition to the Old Testament, which was regarded as sufficient. The Old Testament was the Scripture of Jesus, as well as early Christians.

A fourth reason was that so long as the original apostles lived, there was no need for written records of the life of Jesus. They had been commissioned to preach and evangelize, not to write. Christianity was born into a non-literary situation.

There were four reasons why the church was unlikely to produce books.

First, it was more natural, at least to the Jews, to transmit knowledge orally than to commit it to writing. The great majority of the early Christians did not come from educated circles.

Second, the high cost of writing materials made the possession of written documents difficult or impossible for poor Galilean peasants. By the middle of the first century, such material became necessary. Why? The disciples were dying and unless the story of Christ was fixed in written form, there was every reason to believe that it would become corrupted by omissions, exaggerations, or interpolations.

Third, the spread of the Church itself made the Church unlikely to produce books. Christianity had expanded so far and wide that it necessitated a common message from the firsthand witnesses. It did not appear that the imminent return of the Lord was going to be as immediate as expected. Thus books, which seemed irrelevant to begin with, became of great importance for the teaching of the facts of the Gospel story and the explanation of Christian doctrines and ethics.

Fourth, written documents became a necessity because local churches inevitably found themselves in situations which were puzzling and difficult. Without authoritative documents, confusion would result. In other words, it was put into writing to combat heresy (unorthodox beliefs conflicting with accepted teachings). Between eight or nine different writers contributed to the New Testament; four of them, Matthew, John, Peter, and Paul, were apostles.

Two of them, James and Jude, were half-brothers of Jesus. Luke was a Gentile and the second largest contributor to the New Testament. Mark was a companion of Peter and at various times an assistant to Paul. The identity of the author of the epistle to the Hebrews is uncertain.

Permeating their writings is an inner conviction that these documents are authoritative for the Church because God himself is their source. Christ promised by saying He would empower the apostles to be His witnesses. It was written at a time when the *Koine* Greek language, which was the international language of the Roman Empire, was virtually worldwide.

CANON OF THE NEW TESTAMENT

The New Testament canon is the collection of 27 early Christian writings which, together with the Old Testament canon, is recognized by the Church as its Holy Scripture, containing the final, authoritative deposit of divine revelation. These writings, known as "canon," are normative for every aspect of the life of the Church, be it creed, worship, or its life in the world.

It is vitally important to know when, where, and why the New Testament canon came to be united with the Old Testament canon as Holy Scripture. Why did just these 27 books—out of the vast amount of early Christian writings—come to be received as divinely authoritative?

The first official recognition of the 27 books of the New Testament canon—as being the New Testament canon for the Church—did not occur until A.D. 367.

THE FORMATION OF THE CANON OF THE NEW TESTAMENT

The New Testament, as we now possess it, consists of 27 books. How did these 27 books—and these only—come to be considered our New Testament? Did the Church create the New Testament or did the New Testament create the Church?

Is a New Testament book in the canon because it is authoritative, or is it authoritative because it is in the

Is a New Testament book in the canon because it is authoritative, or is it authoritative because it is in the canon?

canon? What one basic criterion determined a book's acceptance into the canon?

Such questions as these should make obvious the importance of understanding the formation of the New Testament canon.

The word "canon" comes from the Greek word "Kanon," and it is closely related to the Hebrew word for "reed." It has at least three meanings: 1) Literally, it means a straight rod or bar. 2) Metaphorically, it means: "That which serves to measure," that is, a norm or standard. 3) Passively, it denotes that which has been measured and accepted.

In the New Testament, the word "canon" occurs only four times. 2 Corinthians 10:13,14,15. (Here it refers to the province marked off for Paul.) It occurs in Galatians 6:16 (it refers to the standard according to which Paul wanted Christians to walk.)

Thus, Scripture is defined by the rule of the Christian Church, and that which is measured becomes the rule of the church for other cases. The earliest application of the term "canon" to Scripture was by Athanasius in A.D. 350. During the early years of its existence, the church's authority lay primarily in the spoken evidence of eyewitnesses and in the witness of its life.

When a community had received the spoken account of the Gospel message, the need for an authoritative written interpretation of the facts in the life of Christ, together with their application to life, became apparent. For the most part, the Epistles were written to meet this need. The need for authentic accounts of the life of Christ soon became apparent. The Gospels were written to supply this need.

The Book of Acts met the need for an authentic history of the apostolic period, and at the same time showed how Jesus continued His ministry through His followers by the power of the Holy Spirit through the Church.

The Apocalypse was written to set forth God's revelation of the consummation of all things. Thus, over a period of 50 years, there appeared the inspired and authoritative literature which we know as the New Testament and which the Church used alongside the Old Testament.

The formation of the Canon (the books actually included) was a gradual growth. We must note that Christianity was a far-flung international faith and did not have the benefit of a tightly knit prophetic community that could readily keep track of inspired writings.

The earliest letters of the Apostles date from approximately A.D. 50. When Peter and Paul were martyred around A.D. 67, the church was jolted into a new concern for apostolic writings. Though not officially recognized, the entire New Testament had been written by the end of the first century.

As early as A.D. 95, Clement, Bishop of Rome, referred to books, such as Matthew, Luke, and Romans, 1 Corinthians, and Hebrew, as Scripture. It is also important to note that the bulk of the New Testament was accepted by the same generation of believers who had seen Christ at work and who lived in the region of the empty tomb.

The first books to form a collection were probably the letters of Paul. Even within the New Testament itself, there is proof that they existed as a collection and that they were well known.

Peter, in 2 Peter 3:16, referred to them as if they were perfectly familiar to his readers. It is clear that the letters of Paul had been collected and widely known and widely accepted before the end of the first century.

About the same time as the collection of the epistles of Paul, there was a collection of the four Gospels. These Gospels had a ring of truth and the Spirit of God about them.

The church fathers of the first two Christian centuries were unanimous in ascribing authority to these four Gospels, and only to them.

How did church leaders decide which books belong in the canon and which books did not?

FIVE CRITERIA THAT THE EARLY CHURCH USED TO DETERMINE SCRIPTURE

1. **The Test of Apostolicity**: Was the book the work of an apostle, or, if not, did it have an Apostle as its authority?

2. **The Test of Universality:** Was the writing widely circulated and approved by Christians in general?

3. **The Test of Doctrinal Content:** No book was admitted which taught anything contrary to the rule of faith. On the basis of this test, most of the apocryphal books were eliminated.

4. **Test of Intrinsic Worth:** That is the spirituality and sublimity of the books. This does not mean that the books were simply inspiring and worthwhile to read, but they had a dynamic power to transform human life.

5. **The Test of Inspiration:** Did the book give evidence of being divinely inspired? This was the ultimate criterion of canonicity. Everything finally had to give way to it.

An important observation not to be overlooked is that the formation of the canon was a process shaped and guided by the Providence of God. In other words, God who inspired the writings, also had a hand in the selection of His Books over those that were non-inspired writings.

The New Testament came to us naturally, with minimal interference by man. It marched relentlessly through history with such orderly progression that it is tough to quarrel with its claim of divine inspiration.

Thus, the Holy Spirit quickened the instincts of devout men, aided discernment between the genuine and the spurious, and thus led to gradual, harmonious and, in the end, unanimous conclusions. The Holy Spirit not only inspired the writings of the books, He inspired the selection of the books.

A clear reading of the New Testament reveals that the authors themselves assumed a canonical authority. In other words, they understood themselves to be under the inspiration of the Holy Spirit.

It is vital to remember that being accepted into the canon did not elevate a book to Scripture. It simply recognized that the book already was Scripture.

It has been well said that the Bible is not an authorized collection of books, but a collection of authorized books.

THREE SIGNIFICANT FACTORS INFLUENCED THE FORMATION OF THE CANON

THE INFLUENCE OF HERESY

Jesus had warned the Church to be on the lookout for false prophets and teachers, both of whom abounded during the first century (Galatians 1:7ff; 2 Corinthians 11:1-4; 2 Peter 3:1ff).

According to 2 Timothy 3:16-17, all Scripture was to be profitable for teaching doctrine. Thus, it was crucial that each book be seriously evaluated so that false writings could be thrown out once and for all.

A heretic name Marcion, who lived in the middle of the second century, played a key role in stimulating work on the canon.

Marcion published his own canon, which was radical. It made the church realize that action was needed. Marcion had tossed out everything but Luke and 10 of Paul's epistles. Orthodox Christianity said that Marcion's canon was not the true canon.

PERSECUTION

In the year A.D. 303, Emperor Diocletian ordered that all sacred books be destroyed by fire. During this time, Christians naturally guarded canonical books with greater care.

CHRISTIAN WORSHIP

Another factor that influenced the Church to formulate a canon was which books might be read in churches along with books of the Old Testament. Books that were commonly read and used in church worship had a special position, which began their process of entry into the canon.

WHO DECIDED WHICH BOOKS BELONGED TO THE CANON?

The earliest decree of any church council regarding the complete canon was made at the Council of Hippo in A.D. 393. The wording of the resolution is significant: "Besides the canonical scriptures, nothing shall be read in the church under the title of Divine Writings. The canonical books are...." Both the Old and New Testament books are listed.

It is clear that the Council of Hippo did not in any sense create the canon. Rather, the statement assumes that the canon already existed and was recognized and the Council of Hippo merely confirmed the prevailing opinion of the churches. (Remember Athanasius A.D. 367: Clement of Rome A.D. 200 used the term "New Testament," thus formally recognizing it had the same quality of inspiration as the Old Testament.)

Two such lists of authoritative books were compiled in the early church.

The first was Marcion's Canon in the year A.D. 140. His canon was determined by Gnostic tendencies and an anti-Jewish attitude.

Marcion's canon completely disregarded the Old Testament.

We must remember that the Old Testament consisted of three parts: the Law, the Prophets, and the Writings. In the place of the Law, Marcion put the Gospel. He rejected

Matthew, Mark, and John as being far too much influenced by Judaism. I their place he substituted and edited the version of Luke. Every Old Testament reference was deleted.

In place of the Prophets, he substituted the apostle in which he included 10 letters of Paul, whom he regarded as the great enemy of the Old Law and the great exponent of the new Gospel.

The 10 letters were Galatians, 1 and 2 Corinthians, Romans, 1 and 2 Thessalonians, Laodiceans, Colossians, Philippians, and Philemon. The epistle to the Laodiceans is actually Paul's letter to the Ephesians, but Marcion argued from Colossians 4:16 that Ephesians was actually written to Laodicea. For the writings, he substituted a book of his own called the "Antitheses," in which he compiled a list of Old Testament passages with the New Testament contradictions of them.

The list, which was compiled in reaction to Marcion's canon, is known as the "Muratorian Fragment." It dates from around the year A.D. 170 and derives its name from Muratori, an Italian who discovered the Fragment in the Ambrosian Library in Milan in 1740.

The Muratorian Canon is damaged at the beginning, and actually begins with Luke; however, it refers to Luke as the Third Gospel. That being true, we find all the books of our New Testament mentioned except 1 John, 1 and 2 Peter, James, and Hebrews. However, 1 John is quoted in another place in the document. Early on, 1, 2, and 3 John were often considered either one or two letters.

An interesting feature of the Muratorian Fragment is the fact that it refers to the book of Acts as the Acts of All Apostles. This was a reaction against Marcion who, in his view of Paul as the supreme figure in the Church, rejected the Books of Acts.

A document known as the "Diatessaron," written by Tatian around A.D. 170, weaved the Four Gospels into one Gospel. While popular for a short time, the Church unhesitatingly turned away from any attempt to turn them into one.

By the end of the second century, the great centers of the Church were in conscious possession of a New Testament.

The origin of Alexandria (182-251 A.D.) distinguished between the Homogoumena (the universally accepted books) and the Antilegomena (the ones more or less disputed).

There were still discussions on such books as Barnabas, Hermas and the Didache, Hebrews, 2 Peter, 2 and 3 John, James, and Jude.

> By the end of the second century, the great centers of the Church were in conscious possession of a New Testament.

Eusebius of Caesarea (265 to 340 A.D.) added a third classification.

Notha (designating those books which are to be definitely rejected).

His list of disputed books was James, Jude, 2 Peter, and 3 John. However, he declared that the majority accepted these books and he himself seems to have accepted them all.

His NOTHA list included acts of Paul, the Shepherd of Hermas, the Apocalypse of Peter, the Letter of Barnabas, and the Didache.

It should be noted that no one questioned the value of books that bore the names of James, Peter, John, and Jude. The question was, did they actually write them? Test of Apostolicity.

James was debated because its emphasis upon works seemed to contradict Paul's teaching on Justification by faith.

Hebrews came under scrutiny because no mention is made of its author and because it differs in vocabulary and style from the recognized epistles of Paul.

2 Peter seemed to have a different style than 1 Peter. Jude was questioned because it was thought to quote from apocryphal books.

The period from 325 to 400 A.D. is characterized by specific pronouncements, both by individuals and church councils.

The most prominent was by Athanasius, Bishop of Alexandria, in his Easter letter of 367 in which he listed the exact 27 books that we have today.

Shortly after Athanasius, Jerome and Augustine defined that canon by listing the same 27 books.

The Council of Hippo in 393 confirmed the 27 books as the New Testament.

During the Reformation in 1546, the question of canon was re-opened at the Council of Trent: the Roman Catholic Church confirmed the Old and New Testament and then pronounced a curse upon anyone who did not accept this list. In its list, the books included a number of the Apocryphal Writings.

THE NEW TESTAMENT FROM THE SECOND CENTURY FORWARD FROM PRIMITIVE CHURCH TO A.D. 140

This was a time when individual books were known and disseminated. Even though a collection of documents was forming, it is not yet proper to speak of them as canon. Recognition - (internal value, apostolic origin). Affirmation - (by the Church acting officially). Pauline Collection - (2 Peter 3:16 - assumes familiarity with Pauline Collection Gospels - evidence for growing acceptance from quotes from Barn and 2 Clem.)

FROM A.D. 140 TO 180

This was a second main period in the development of a canon due to leading personalities. The Place of Marcion (Gnostic was expelled from church by 144 A.D.). He denied that the Old Testament and New Testament God were the same (Gospel and apostle sections of Paul and only Luke). Just Martyr. (All four Gospels, apocalypse, Paul mentioned with Hebrew and Acts.)

FROM A.D. 180

Ireneus. Against heresies, (22/27; Gospels, Acts 13 Paul, 1 Peter 1 and 2, John, Apocalypse). Muratorian Fragment. (Discovered 1740 by Muratori) gives details about author, destination, origin, and purpose of books. (22/27 missing Hebrews, ? Peter, 2 John and James. Origin (185-255) - three classes of Scriptures - "Acknowledged"—no dispute about four Gospels; 13 Paul; 1 Peter; 1 John; Acts; and Revelation. "Disputed" 2 Peter; 2/3 John, Hebrews; Barn; and Didache. "False" heretical gospels being circulated. Athanasius letter of 367 A.D.; also Vulgate and Third Council of Carthage (397). Martin Luther saw Hebrew, James, Jude, and Revelation as inferior.

STUDY QUESTIONS

1. What is Revelation?
2. What is Inspiration?
3. What is Inerrancy?
4. What is Textual Criticism?
5. What are Autographs?
6. What are Manuscripts?
7. What does the term "canon" mean?
8. List the five criteria used to determine Scripture.

Chapter Six

WHY I BELIEVE THAT JESUS IS GOD

GOD WAS IN CHRIST RECONCILING THE WORLD UNTO himself" (2 Corinthians 5:19).

"In the beginning was the Word and the Word was with God and the Word was God, the same was in the beginning with God all things were made by Him and not anything that was made was made.... And the Word became flesh and dwelt among us and we beheld his glory..." (John 1:1-4; 14).

The New Testament makes the claim that Jesus was God—that He existed in eternity past with the Father and the Spirit. Everything owes its existence to the uncreated Word of God. The Word had the same nature that God had; He was spirit (John 4:24).

To deny the deity of Christ as God is to destroy the foundation of the Christian faith. It is the belief that essentially and clearly distinguishes Christians from non-Christians. It is the reason for everything else. Christians believe that Christ is divine; his authority is supreme and infallible. Christianity is not a philosophy but a religion. It rests first of all not on human reason but on divine revelation.

The modern skeptic or atheist will appreciate Jesus for what He said about others and how they should live, but ignore what He said about himself.

If Jesus is in fact God and man, then He reveals to us in a final and exhaustive way both who God is and who we are. The modern skeptic or atheist will appreciate Jesus for what He said about others and how they should live, but ignore what He said about himself.

THE CLAIMS OF CHRIST

What did Jesus really say about himself? Was He just a prophet or wise man? Was He just a good moral philosopher or ethicist? Or was He in fact God manifested in human flesh?

First, Jesus claimed that He had the power to forgive sins (Mark 5:12; Luke 24:45-47). No one had the power to forgive sins but God alone.

Second, Jesus also claimed that He was sinless (John 8:46). He said to his critics, which of you convicts me of sin? He lived a sinless life.

Third, He performed many miracles. He raised the dead (John 11) and even rose from the dead himself (Matthew 27-28). It is interesting to read that the Gospel accounts of the miracles that Jesus performed. The Pharisees and the Sadducees never questioned whether the miracles were authentic or genuine. Their issues of contention were to the source or origin of Jesus's power, believing that it was of demonic origin.

Fourth, He accepted the title from Thomas (John 20:28): *"My Lord and My God"* and accepted his worship of Him. Jesus claimed that He had the power to bestow eternal life on those who would believe in Him (John 3:16; 5:39-40). Jesus could foretell and predict the future (Matthew 24; Luke 241-7; John 6:64).

Jesus is either God, if His claims about himself are true, or He is a bad man, if what He said was not true, for good men do not claim to be God. But Jesus was not a bad man. If anyone in history was not a bad man, Jesus was not a bad man. Therefore, He was and is God.

Jesus is either Lord or sovereign ruler of the universe—or He is the greatest liar who ever lived, and millions of people have been duped by a sham. Or Jesus was a lunatic and was completely out of His mind. He was disillusioned.

OLD TESTAMENT TESTIMONY

The fact that Jesus claimed to be God is derived by what He said and did.

The fact that Jesus claimed to be God is derived by what He said and did. In the Old Testament, the Jews would never refer to God by His name or even write his name. Because the Jews would not pronounce His name scholars today suggest that in the Hebrew text there are four consonants (YHWH) in our English Bible translated as "Lord" or "Jehovah" and believed to be the special name given by God Himself.

In Exodus 3:14, God says, "I Am WHO I AM." (Yahweh) refers only to God himself. In John 17:5, Jesus prayed, "And now, O Father, glorify thou me with thine own self with the glory which I had with thee before the world was." But in Isaiah 42:8, Yahweh of the Old Testament said, "My glory will I not give to another." Jesus said also in John 8:58: "Before Abraham was, I AM." Jesus claims not only that He existed before Abraham, but equality with the "I AM" in Exodus 3:4.

The Jews clearly understood what Jesus had said and picked up stones to kill him for blasphemy. Jesus claimed for himself divine prerogatives of God. Jesus is equal to God the Father in His divine nature, but subordinate in His human nature. He is equal to God in His divine essence, but subordinate in His human function. He is equal to God in His divine attributes, but subordinate in His human office. And Jesus is equal to God the Father in His divine character, but subordinate in His human position.

IS JESUS THE ONLY WAY?

Philip Graham Ryken in his book, *Is Jesus the Only Way?* (1999), details for us the post-Christian America we live in. He develops the idea of pluralism as a social, religious, and political ideology. Ryken discusses three types of pluralism. The first pluralism is empirical pluralism, by which he means the fact of living in a diverse society. America is a country of many languages, ethnicity, religions, and world views. The second pluralism is cherished pluralism. Cherished pluralism is to appreciate it, welcome it, celebrate it, and approve it. We do this by having multicultural awareness events. The third kind of pluralism is philosophical pluralism. This is the ideology that refuses to allow any single religion or world view to claim exclusive a hold on the Truth. It denies that there are absolute truths. It insists that all religions and world views must be seen as equally valid because philosophical pluralism is so pervasive.

The question many unbelievers ask is, how can Jesus be the only way? Is Christianity anything more than narrow-minded bigotry? Christianity requires an all-or-nothing commitment to Jesus Christ. Biblical Christianity has always been an exclusive religion. Jesus Christ refuses to have any colleagues. So as believers, he insists that Jesus is the only way we will discover in our post-modern culture which has become increasingly unpopular to take a stand on the uniqueness of Christ. If believers are going to insist that Christianity is true—and all other religions are false—then we have to explain why Christianity is true (1 Peter 3:15).

STUDY QUESTIONS

1. What are the five reasons in the gospels that demonstrate that Jesus was God?
2. What Old Testament Scriptures point to Jesus as God?

Chapter Seven

WHY I BELIEVE IN THE RESURRECTION OF JESUS

T he foundation to which all of Christianity hinges is on the fact of the resurrection. Everything that Jesus said and did hinges upon this critical point to which Christianity rises or falls. There have been many skeptic even to this very day who question the event and the actuality of the resurrection. In this chapter I want to present to the various theories against the resurrection and to show their lack of evidentiary support.

HISTORICAL PROOF

Jesus was seen by at least 500 brethren (1 Corinthians 15:1ff). Luke recorded in Acts 1:1-3 that Jesus presented himself alive with many infallible proofs which many could attest that He did in fact rise from the dead.

THEORIES TO EXPLAIN THE RESURRECTION

THE SWOON THEORY

The swoon theory says when Jesus was crucified, He did not really die but he fainted or went into a deep coma. When they took His body and placed it in the tomb, Joseph of Arimathea placed spices around the body of Jesus. The dampness, the coolness of the tomb, and the spices awakened Jesus out of this deep coma.

John said it was the custom of the Romans that when criminals were crucified, the Roman soldiers would come to see if they were in fact dead. The way they determined this was by breaking their legs, but when they came to Jesus, they discovered He was already dead. They took a spear and pierced Him in the side, and out of His side came blood and water.

If Jesus was in a deep coma and was in a weakened state, He would not have had the strength to move or roll away the stone that sealed the tomb. Because he was on the cross from the sixth to the ninth hour, he would have been too weak.

Crucified criminals died from asphyxiation and dehydration rather than being crucified.

THE DISCIPLES STOLE THE BODY OF JESUS

This theory says that the Christian faith started as a lie and a farce and is built on a lie. The problem with this theory is that sane people do not die for what they know is a lie. They will die for something they believe to be true. But if they knew that Jesus did not rise from the dead, they would not have given their lives.

THE JEWS AND THE ROMAN SOLDIERS STOLE THE BODY OF JESUS

The Romans would have had no reason or interest in the body of Jesus. They were totally objective about the entire ordeal of Jesus's death. If the Jews stole the body, the easiest way to discredit the Christian faith is to present the body of Jesus and say that He did not rise from the dead because here is the body.

THE GREATEST EVIDENCE FOR THE RESURRECTION

THE EMPTY TOMB

We can go to the tomb of every ancient philosopher and teacher who ever lived and discover that the tomb contains the remains of their physical existence. But go to the empty tomb to look for the body of Jesus and we will discover as the angels said to Mary, "He is not here for He has risen from the dead," as He predicted He would do.

THE TESTIMONY OF THE EYEWITNESS

In the powerful testimony of the Church through the preaching of the Gospel, Luke recorded in Acts 8:4: "Those

> The Christian faith that was introduced to the ancient world was such a new phenomenon that it took the ancient world by storm.

who were scattered went everywhere preaching the word." By the end of third century, Christianity had become such a powerful influence in the lives of people that it was soon legalized as an official religion of the Roman empire. The Christian faith that was introduced to the ancient world was such a new phenomenon that it took the ancient world by storm.

THE ESTABLISHMENT OF THE CHURCH

Today, all over the world people believe in the resurrection and worship Him every Sunday as the King of Kings and Lord of Lords from every denomination, creed, ethnicity and gender, the Church becomes a witness to the life, death, and resurrection of Christ.

THE PERSECUTION OF THE CHURCH

People will not be persecuted for something they know is not true—only for something they believe in. Millions of Christians—since the origin of the Christian faith—have been thrown to the lions burned at the stake, beheaded for their faith in Christ. This demonstrates the dramatic and dynamic influence on the lives of believers all over the world.

DOCTRINAL PROOF

The Old Testament predicted the coming of Jesus, his death, burial, and resurrection, according to Isaiah 53, Matthew 12, and Luke 24:44-46.

PERSONAL PROOF

The conversion of Paul on the road to Damascus in Acts 9, 26 convinced him to turn and give his life to Christ. Here was a staunch proponent of Judaism who now radically turned to Christ and began to preach the Gospel that he once tried to destroy.

The conversion of the Corinthians in Acts 18 was done in the dramatic power of the Holy Spirit which was reproduced not only in the life of Paul, but their very lives as well—a changed life—and they were never the same from that day onward.

Every day many believers' lives have been changed from a life of degradation, sin, and humiliation. Those whose lives were strung out on drugs, alcohol, and sex addiction can attest to the power and dynamic change that has occurred since Jesus came into their hearts. The Apostle Paul could attest to the fact in Romans 1:16-17: "For I am not ashamed of the gospel of Christ for it is the power of God unto salvation to everyone who believes to the Jesus first and also unto the Greek, for there is in the righteousness of God is revealed from faith to faith; for the just shall live by faith."

STUDY QUESTIONS

1. What are three reasons given by critics to disprove the resurrection of Jesus?
2. What are the seven reasons the author gives for proof that the resurrection really did happen?
3. What is the Swoon theory?

Chapter Eight

WHY I BELIEVE IN MIRACLES

ONCE THE PREMISE THAT GOD EXISTS IS ACCEPTED, THERE is no problem with the belief in miracles. The question of whether miracles are possible is not a scientific but a philosophical issue. Scientists can only say miracles do not occur in the ordinary cause of nature. Science cannot forbid or exclude miracles because natural laws do not cause and therefore cannot forbid them. Natural laws are merely descriptions of what happens.

The scientific method used by scientists is valid only for realities which can be measurable in physical ways. God exists in a metaphysical reality which is different from the world of nature that science examines. Science can tell us only how something works—not why it works the way it does. The issue of miracles or the miraculous when we pray is a question that goes to the very heart of our belief system. Is our God all powerful? Does our God know the future? Do we believe that the Bible is a supernatural book?

THE DEFINITION OF A MIRACLE

A miracle is defined as anything that is unusual or unexpected and not necessarily that which the hand of God has produced (see counterfeit miracles that Satan can performed in 2 Corinthians 11:12ff). Miracles are the acts of God in which He breaks into human history and changes or interrupts the course of ordinary things. So if God exists,

> The only way to prove that miracles are impossible is to disprove the existence of God.

miracles are possible. If there is a God who can act, then there can be acts of God. The only way to prove that miracles are impossible is to disprove the existence of God. A miracle is something which would have never happened had nature been left to its own devices. Natural laws describe naturally caused regularities. A miracle is a supernaturally caused singularity.

WHAT IS A NATURAL LAW?

A natural law is a general description of an orderly way in which the world operates. It follows that a miracle is an unusual, irregular, specific way in which God acts within the world.

WHY WOULD GOD PERFORM MIRACLES?

The God we serve is the kind of God who desires to do good for His people, and a miracle by definition is an event that does this very thing. Miracles bring healing and restoration and bring back to life. Miracles communicate God's will and vindicate his attributes.

FIVE DIMENSIONS OF MIRACLES

First, miracles have an unusual character. It is a highly unusual event or experience in contrast to the regular pattern of events in the natural world. As a "wonder," it attracts attention by its uniqueness, for example, the burning bush, fire from heaven, walking on water.

Second, miracles have a theological dimension. A miracle is an act of God that presupposes a God who acts.

Third, a miracle has a moral dimension. It brings glory to God by manifesting His moral character. Miracles are invisible acts that reflect the invisible nature of God. Miracles by nature aim to produce and promote good.

Fourth, miracles have a doctrinal dimension. Miracles in the Bible are connected directly and indirectly with "truth claims." They always indicate a false prophet from a true prophet (Deuteronomy 18:22). They confirm the truth of God through the servant of God (Hebrews 2:3-4). Miracles and messages go hand in hand.

Fifth, miracles have a teleological dimension. Unlike magic, they are never performed to entertain (Luke 23:8; Acts 8). Miracles have a distinct purpose to glorify God and to provide evidence for people to believe by affirming the message of God.

God is sovereign in that He can work through general and special providence without suspending natural laws. While the special gift of miracles has ceased, the fact of miracles has not vanished.

STUDY QUESTIONS

1. What is a miracle?
2. What is natural law?
3. What are the five dimensions of a miracle?

Chapter Nine

GOD HAS NOT LEFT HIMSELF WITHOUT A WITNESS

IN ACTS 14:16-17, PAUL AND BARNABAS INSTRUCTED the people in Lystra that "in past generations He (God) allowed all nations to walk in their own ways. Yet he did not leave himself without a witness, for He did good by giving you rains from heaven and fruitful seasons, satisfying your hearts with food and gladness." Paul further makes it emphatically clear that God has not left himself with a witness in His world.

Romans 1:18: "For the wrath of God is revealed from heaven against all ungodliness and unrighteousness of men, who by their unrighteousness suppressed the truth. For what can be known about God is plain to them because God has shown it to them, For His invisible attributes, namely His eternal power and divine nature have been clearly perceived, ever since the creation of the world, in the things that have been made, so they are without excuse." There are seven witnesses that are reveal in the Scriptures which teach us about the nature and character of God.

THE WITNESS OF CONSCIENCE

The word "conscience" is a Latin term con, meaning "with" and science, to know or knowledge. So a conscience is any learned behavior. Thomas Aquinas (1225-1274), the great medieval theologian, described conscience as the inner voice of God by which we are either accused or excused for our actions. It is the internal governor that restrains or allows our behavior. The inner voice of conscience can be muted by an habitual life of sin (1 Timothy 4:1-4).

In Romans 2:15, Paul says that the law of God, His moral law, has been written in the heart of every person, and His law can be suppressed, but it can never be erased (Romans 1:18). It is the voice of God which speaks through the preaching of the word through the convincing

His moral law, has been written in the heart of every person, and His law can be suppressed, but it can never be erased.

power of the Spirit. It awakens the conscience and captures it when it accepts biblical truth. Paul further presses his point by mentioning that every person conscious can become seared to the point that God, by His providential will, cannot penetrate their heart.

THE WITNESS OF GOD-WARD LONGING

St. Augustine (354-430), bishop and theologian, was right when he said, "Our hearts are restless until we find rest in thee." The longing of the human soul for authentic existence can never be satisfied with idols that can never save, but there is the unknown God who can and is seeking for those who want rest (Matthew 11:28). In the hustle and bustle of life, we observed people yearning and trying to find peace and purpose to their existence.

THE WITNESS OF GOD'S HANDIWORK

The glory of God not only shines forth brightly in the brilliance of creation—the heavens (Psalms 19:1-6;104; Acts 14:17), but also the creatures who are made in His image, namely, man (Genesis 1:26-27; 9:6; Psalms 8:1-9; 139:13;114).

THE WITNESS OF THE HARVEST

The Scriptures are replete with the principle that every sin is linked with consequences; whatever we sow, we will reap (Proverbs 1:31; Jeremiah 17:10; Hosea 10:12; Galatians 6:7). In Genesis 8:22, God says as long as the earth remains there will be seed time and harvest. This is a fundamental law that God has built in creation, and this principle works in relationships, finances, spiritual, and physical reproduction.

THE WITNESS OF AN ORDERLY LABOR

From the natural labor of working in the natural realm there emerges an orderly cycle. For example, when the farmer prepares for a new year, he has a system of preparing the soil, planting the seeds, rotating the fields, and harvesting his crops. He knows that at specific times of the year certain tasks must be accomplished if he is going to have a productive year (see, for example, Isaiah 28:23-26).

THE WITNESS OF DESIGN

The witness of design is one of the profoundest arguments for the existence of God. It is called the "teleological argument." When we look at the argument of design from a human perspective, it points to the intentions of God as the Creator and Designer of His creatures, and this is reflected in the "blueprint" of our physical, intellectual, and spiritual nature.

THE WITNESS OF SEXUAL DESIGN

The attack on biblical and traditional values, which have shaped and molded Western culture, is being challenged at its very foundation today. A current movement within our society advances same sex marriages or homosexual unions—sometimes referred to as "civil unions." Devotees advancing the ideas of same-sex marriages are blurring the unique and distinctive roles of male and female relationships. It is clear in Romans 1:26-27 that God has designed male and female for sexual compatibility, enjoyment, and reproductive purposes. Our sexual identity points to a Creator who desires that we express our unique personalities through our sexuality.

STUDY QUESTIONS

1. Why is it so important that God has left a witness of Himself in creation?
2. What does the word "conscience" mean?
3. How does God awaken the "conscience"?

4. How do you understand St. Augustine's statement: "Our hearts are restless until we find rest in thee."

5. What does the witness of Design say to us about our Creator?

Chapter Ten

COME AND LET US REASON TOGETHER

ONE OF THE MOST IMPORTANT TASKS WE CAN DO, AS believers is to confront the culture in which we live and be able to clearly think and present in a persuasive manner the content and credibility of the gospel message. In this section, I want to consider some common mistakes or fallacies that most people make when presenting their arguments as to why they are for or against something. It amazes me when talking about a biblical matter that most people do not appeal to reasonable and logical thinking, but rather to their emotions or traditions.

In this section I rely on Arlie J. Hoover's book the *Fallacies of Unbelief* (1976) in which he does a masterful job pointing out common assumption that people have without really giving serious critical analysis to their current belief systems.

THE FALLACY OF FIDEISM

Fideism is the belief that one does not have to use reason to believe something is valid for his faith. But the Scriptures admonish us, as believers, to use our minds (see 1 Thessalonians 5:21; 1 Corinthians 10:15; Philippians 1:9; Ephesians 1:17,18; Romans 1:19,20; John 4:24; Matthew 13:19; Luke 10:27).

THE FALLACY OF RATIONALISM

Rationalism considers all forms of faith to be irrational. Faith is considered to be blind, a leap in the darkness, and that we only need to use our reason and intellectual powers to solve moral and social problems. The problem with rationalism—devoid of biblical truth—is that human reason has nothing in which to evaluate truth. Many moral injustices have been perpetrated upon the human race by those who have rationalized and justified their actions. . Human reasoning is limited to four major areas. First, human reasoning cannot make the knowledge of God real to unregenerate people. Second, reasoning cannot yield a supernatural revelation or even "sense" it by mere reasons. Third, human reasoning does not receive divine revelation, therefore it cannot determine what that revelation may or may not contain. Fourth, human reasoning cannot apprehend divine revelation as divine revelation, but it may recognize its presence.

THE FALLACY OF REDUCTIONISM

The fallacy of reductionism is reducing something complex to being merely the sum of its parts. When we say that something is complicated is "merely" or "nothing but" "this" or "that" is limiting to that object or person. For example of the fallacy of reductionism are when women say that "all men are dogs," or men say that "women cannot think."

THE FALLACY OF GENETICS

The fallacy of genetics is the ideology of demeaning something or belittling it just because of its humble beginnings. The problem with the genetic fallacy is that it overlooks the facts of human experience. Many great and wonderful things in life begin from very humble beginnings. Anything or anyone who grows, changes, or improves is obviously going to outrun its origin, and any observation made of it must correspond to its present status, not its beginning, as seen in John 1:43-51. John records the calling of the first disciples in the public ministry of Jesus. When Phillip found Nathaniel, he told him he had found the Messiah. Nathaniel wanted to know where the Messiah came from. When he was told the Messiah came from Nazareth, Nathaniel replied, "Can anything good come out of Nazareth?" This is a classic example of the genetic fallacy.

THE FALLACY OF SPECIAL PLEADING

The fallacy of special pleading is dramatizing the material or highlighting the material that confirms your position and ignores or belittles the material that disapproves your position.

THE FALLACY OF THE MISUSE OF ANALOGY

The fallacy of the misuse of analogy deals with the premise that you try to prove too much from a comparison of two things that are similar. You draw false inference based on the comparisons of things that are similar.

THE FALLACY OF A FAULTY DILEMMA

A dilemma is defined as having just two choices in a situation, both of them are usually bad. This is sometimes referred to as being "on the horns of a dilemma." A faulty dilemma is when you suppose there are only two choices, when, in fact, there may be three or more choices. When you find a third choice, it is called "slipping between the horns."

THE FALLACY OF CHRONOLOGICAL SNOBBERY

The fallacy of chronological snobbery is refuting an idea or issue merely by dating it, usually by dating it as being very old. You are quick to say that something is out of date. The assumption is something is false just because it is old and something true because it is new. Age is not a criterion for truth.

THE FALLACY OF POISONING THE WELL

This fallacy of poisoning the well deals with the premise of discrediting a source of evidence in advance. When you attack the person who is presenting the evidence, it is called the ad hominen fallacy. The term ad hominen is a Latin term meaning "to discredit the man and you will discredit his evidence or position."

THE FALLACY OF EXTENSION

The fallacy of extension deals with the true intentions of the debater who wants to win his argument by interpreting his opponent's position in the worse possible light. He extends his opponent's position when he exaggerates his ideas into a form he can easily destroy. His extension is a distortion though it may retain the core of his opponent's original position.

THE FALLACY OF ARGUMENT TO IGNORANCE

The fallacy of argument to ignorance stipulates that one is given only two positions on an issue. The opposing adversary positions wins by default. His opponent cannot establish his position because he is ignorant of the information that will help him make his argument. He feels he has won the argument when, in fact, he has won the debate. But his position is wrong because his opponent was not aware of the necessary information that could have helped him in his defense.

THE FALLACY ADDRESSED TO MISERY

The fallacy addressed to misery deals with feelings having no logical relation to the issue being discussed.

THE FALLACY OF THE MISUSE OF AUTHORITY

The fallacy of the misuse of authority occurs when we make an illegitimate use of an authority. This fallacy is achieved in two fundamental ways: First, you may choose to cite an authority or expert on an issue that may be totally unrelated to his field of competence. Second, when you cite an expert or authority, you should never assume that he is infallible. A subtle form of the misuse of authority is the testimonials used in television commercials for the plausibility and proof of the quality of a given product that the authority person has been hired to promote.

THE FALLACY OF THE MISUSE OF EMOTIONAL WORDS

In the heat of an argument we use words that speak of our feelings more so than about our logic, for example, screaming at the opponent and calling him foolish.

STUDY QUESTIONS

1. What reason does the author cite as to why it is important to think clearly?
2. Define the term "fideism."
3. Define the term "rationalism."
4. Define the term "reductionism."
5. What is the fallacy of genetics ?
6. What is the fallacy of special pleading?
7. What is the fallacy of the misuse of analogy?
8. What is the fallacy of a faulty dilemma?
9. Give an example of the fallacy of chronological snobbery.
10. Give an illustration of the fallacy of poisoning the well.
11. What is the fallacy of extension?
12. What is the fallacy of argument to ignorance?
13. Give an example of the fallacy addressed to misuse.

14. Give an illustration of the fallacy of the misuse of authority.

15. What is the fallacy of the misuse of emotional words?

Chapter Eleven

BELIEF SYSTEMS

S A BELIEVER, YOU WILL ENCOUNTER ON A DAILY basis—
at work, on your travels, through the media—many
different belief systems that flatly contradict the
biblical world view. Having a tool to classify and label these
various belief systems will aid you to clarify what you read
and hear. In this chapter, I want to highlight some belief
systems that are adverse to the Christian faith. St.
Augustine said that "you should never judge a belief or
philosophy by its abuse." The theologian meant that the
truthfulness of a belief is not predicated on how well people
may or may not behave, but that it should be judged by the
truth claims. Every philosophy and belief system, as well
Christianity, should be examined and judged based on the
truth of its claims that can be tested.

CRITERIA FOR EXAMINING BELIEF SYSTEMS

The believer has five key ways to test any belief system or statement that makes a claim to truth. First, is the belief statement logically consistent? Is there coherence, clarity, and lack of contradictions within the belief system? Second, is the belief system empirically sufficient? Can the truth claims be verified by the senses (seeing, tasting, touching, smelling, hearing)? Third, is the belief system experientially relevant? Does the belief system apply meaningfully to your life? Fourth, is the belief system undeniable? For example, although your existence cannot be proven logically, it is nevertheless existentially undeniable. You cannot deny your existence without affirming it at the same time. Fifth, is the belief system unaffirmable? Just because something can be stated does not necessarily follow that the statement is true. For example, you cannot say that you do not speak English and affirm at the same time you are speaking English. The statement is therefore false.

QUESTIONS THAT TRUTH SHOULD ANSWER

The ultimate question of truth deals with four fundamental question: What is the origin of human life? What is the meaning of human life? What is the morality of human living? And what is the destiny of the human soul? No thinking person can avoid these questions in his search for truth which can end only when one is convinced that the answers espoused are true.

SECULARISM

Historically, the word "secular" was a positive word in the church's vocabulary. The word "secular" has its origin and roots in Latin and comes from the word *Saeculum*, which means "world." Another Latin word for "world" is *Mundus*. Since both words, *Saeculum* and *Mundus*, mean "world," what is the difference? The people who lived in the ancient world understood that, as human beings, they lived in time and space. Our lives are both spatial and geographical. We live in a time frame—this age. So in Latin the word for this world, in terms of time, is *saeculum*. The word for this world, in terms of space, is *mundus*. So the term "secular" refers then to the world of time. Its focus and emphasis are upon the here and now. The accent of the secular is on the recent time rather than on eternity. You live right now. Because we are time-bound creatures, we plan for tomorrow, but tomorrow is not certain because we live in the world of time.

The philosophy of secularism says the only time we have now is all the time we have. But the biblical view of time is radically different from secular time: After this time there is a world of eternity that we all must face. According to secularism, all of life's activities and relationships must be understood in the light of the present time.

HUMANISM

Humanism has its beginning in Ancient Greece with the pre-Socratic philosopher Protagoras (480-411 BC). Protagoras developed a concept of humanism, which he set forth under the motto *homo mensura*, "Man is the measure of all things." Man, in himself, is the ultimate norm by which all values are to be determined. He is the ultimate being and the ultimate authority, and all reality centers around him. The humanist's creed is: the natural world is the only one we can know; the here-and-now is all there is; insight, intuition, and divine revelation must be tested by reason; truth is best discovered rationally; mankind is the only source of morals and values, and the highest human achievement is to improve the human condition; the future will be better if people proceed ethically and rationally; democracy in all aspects of life is to be strived for, as a means of enhancing personal freedom.

NARCISSISM

Today, we live in one of the most narcissistic cultures of all time. In Greek mythology, Narcissus saw a reflection of himself in the clear water of a pond and fell in love with his own image. What he did was mythical. What we do is real. People today are so infatuated with themselves. Billions of dollars are spent on the cosmetic industry. The heath and fitness craze we see on television dominates our lives. Narcissism is the belief in self-infatuation or self-importance.

RELATIVISM

Relativism is based on the philosophy of pluralism, that is, we have diversity in the world. We have no access to ultimate truth, therefore there are no absolute truths. All truth is relative.

MATERIALISM

Materialism is the belief that the meaning of life can be found only in personal possessions. People are working two and three jobs to acquire more material possessions or creature comforts. But joy is not found in things—but in a relationship with the living God.

PRAGMATISM

Pragmatism is the philosophy of problem-solving. Devotees of pragmatism ask specific questions. Does it work? What brings the best results? Modern man today looks to science, education, and government to solve his problems. He does not look to God to solve his problems. Pragmatism shares the skepticism of secularism about the realm of the supernatural. Knowledge of the supernatural is closed out to us. The pragmatist is concerned only about the present. The pragmatist's view of truth is: "Truth is that which works the good is that which works." The problem with pragmatism is that when some things works for you, it might not work for me. Which one of us is right? According to the pragmatist, both of us are right. So truth for the pragmatist is relative. There is no ultimate standard of truth. The only test for truth is the individual himself.

ANTI-INTELLECTUALISM

Anti-intellectualism espouses mindlessness or the dumbing down of popular culture. It is the shrinking of the mind. People no longer want to read and think; they simply what to be entertained and to feel good.

NEO-PAGANISM

Neo-paganism is the revival of ancient paganism that existed in Ancient Greece and Rome. Neo-paganism has several major components that have striking similarity to modern culture. First, neo-paganism espouses a belief in polytheism, which is the death of monotheism and the belief in one God that Paul so well articulated in Athens in the first century. Second, neo-paganism involves witchcraft. Because neo-paganism is so diverse in terms of polytheism, each devotee is allowed to worship any god or goddess, ancient or modern, from east to west. Neo-paganism believes in a spiritual world, but that world is controlled by occultism, which is the belief in impersonal forces, energy, or power in which they can do supernatural things.

HEDONISM

Hedonism is the belief that good and evil are defined in terms of pleasure and pain. Man's ultimate purpose for living is to be found in enjoying pleasure and avoiding pain. Hedonism seeks pleasure strictly on the level of sensual feelings. The hedonist philosophy is: "If it feels good, then do it." The hedonist creed is: "Eat , drink, and be merry, for tomorrow we die."

EXISTENTIALISM

In its most basic definition existentialism is a philosophy about human existence. It views a person not in terms of his mind or soul, but of his will and his feelings. Man is a crea-ture of passion. He feels strongly. He cares about life. He cries, sighs, and yearns to fulfill his aspirations. Existentialism is always expressed not by what you think but by what you feel. The test for objective truth cannot be based on how one may feel.

LOGICAL POSITIVISM

Logical positivism is a philosophy that tries to establish rules of meaning—how we describe whether something is meaningful or not. Positivism seeks to established the Law of Verification. This law, simply stated, is: "No statement is meaningful unless it can be verified empirically." To verify something means to show that it is true. How can we verify the truth of a statement? To verify a statement, we must use our senses of taste, touch, smell, hearing, and seeing. The problem with the Law of Verification is that it is too narrow and too restrictive. For example, statements such as "I love you" cannot be verified empirically, but people consider it to be meaningful. But this law has another major problem, which is self-contradictory: in order for them to be true, all statements must be verified empirically. Then the Law of Verification is also a meaningless statement because it can not be verified empirically as well.

STUDY QUESTIONS

1. How does the author define a "belief system"?
2. Why does the author say that a "philosophy" or "belief system" should not be judged by its "abuses" rather than in the merits of the philosophy?
3. What are the five criteria for examining any belief system?

4. What are the four fundamental questions that a "truth claim" should answer?

5. Define the term "humanism."

6. Give an illustration of narcissistic behavior.

7. Define the term "relativism."

8. What is the definition of "materialism"?

9. Give an example of the philosophy of pragmatism.

10. What is anti-intellectualism?

11. Define and illustrate the belief of neo-paganism.

12. Give an example of hedonism.

13. What is the philosophy of existentialism?

14. Why is logical positivism a self-contradictory philosophy?

Chapter Twelve

APOLOGETIC PREACHING

I T IS VITAL AND CRITICAL IN A POST-MODERN, AND PLURAL-istic culture for the church, through her preaching, to provide a clear and definable distinction between the various secular and humanist philosophies that are in circulation. When the church is apologetic in her preaching, it develops believers within the church who are able to better give a consistent and rational explanation of their faith.

But two very important questions must be asked in order to develop an effective preaching program. First, how is apologetics related to the preaching event? Second, is there a difference between evangelistic preaching and apologetic preaching?

THE ROLE OF APOLOGETICS IN PREACHING

There are six key elements in developing an effective apologetics for the preaching event. First, apologetics must identify those points of contacts that will aid in the effective delivery and presentation of the gospel to reduce barriers in the life of the unbeliever. Second, apologetics allow the preacher to proclaim the gospel in the experiential world of unbelievers. Apologetics gives the preacher the ability to relate the gospel to the needs of the unbeliever. Third, apologetics afford the preacher the ability to anticipate and answer some of the obstacles to faith that are experienced within the audience on Sunday morning. Fourth, apologetics preaching will challenge the existing non-Christians world views present within the audience on Sunday. Fifth, apologetics preaching creates an intellectual atmosphere favorable for creating faith in the unbeliever. And sixth, apologetics preaching can explain how an unbeliever can become a believer in Christ.

KEY ELEMENTS IN AN APOLOGETICS SERMON

Several vital keys are needed to build and deliver an apologetics sermon. First, anticipate the difficulties that believers in your congregation will have and how they can be handled. These difficulties could take the following format: anticipate questions by unbelievers; show concern about their anxiety about the goodness of God; make a list of difficulties, potential or real; and work through them over the course of a year. Second, explain basic ideas and concepts of the Christian faith in order for believers to develop a greater understanding. The best defense of the Christian faith lies in its explanation Third, reassure believers of the credibility of the Christian faith. Apologetics function within the life of the church from different perspectives, objective and subjective. Objective apologetics reassure those inside the church of the credibility of the Christian faith. Subjective apologetics attempt to create a climate of credibility in which believers come to feel good about their faith. It seeks to build up the confidence of the church that will nourish the ministry of evangelism.

APOLOGETICS AND EVANGELISM

When intellectual reasons have been presented for the credibility of the Christian faith, the unbeliever's objections have now been answered, and then the transition of witnessing to the unbeliever can now be done without further

The task of apologetics is to make the job of evangelism much easier to proclaim Christ and not to defend Christ.

barriers. The task of apologetics is to make the job of evangelism much easier to proclaim Christ and not to defend Christ. As we continue to live in a pluralistic society, will you be set for the defense!

STUDY QUESTIONS

1. How can you as a Bible schoolteacher, minister or elder prepare your students and members in your preaching and teaching to give solid answers for their faith?

2. Why is so important that you make a clear distinction between what the Christian faith teaches from other secular world views?

FURTHER READING

Boyd, Gregory A.. *Letters from a Skeptic.*

Brown, Colin, *Miracles and the Critical.*

Cowan, Stephen B.. *Five Views of Apologetics.*

Craig, Williams L. *God? A debate between a Christian an Atheist.*

Craig, Williams L. *Reasonable Faith: Christian Truth and Apologetics.*

Geisler, Norman. *Why I Am a Christian.*

Geisler, Norman. *Introduction to Philosophy.*

Geisler, Norman. *Christian Apologetics.*

Geisler, Norman. *Answering Islam.*

Geisler, Norman. *Baker Encyclopedia of Christian Apologetics.*

Hart, Trevor. *Faith Thinking: The Dynamics of Christian Theology.*

Hoover, Arlie. *Fallacies of Unbelief.*

Kumar, Steve. *Christianity for Skeptics.*

Lewis, C.S. *Mere Christianity.*

Little, Paul. *Know Why You Believe.*

Muncaster, Ralph O. *Creation versus Evolution.*

Ryken, Philip, Graham. *Is Jesus the Only Way?*

Sproul, R.C. *Defending Your Faith.*

Sproul, R.C. *The Consequences of Ideas.*

Sproul, R.C. *Life Views.*

Sproul, R.C. *Not a Chance.*

Sproul, R.C. *Tearing Down Strongholds.*

Stobel, Lee. *The Case for Christ.*

Zacharias, Ravi. *Jesus Among Other Gods.*

Zacharias, Ravi. *Light in the Shadow of Jihad.*

Zacharias, Ravi. *Can Man Live without God?*

Zacharias, Ravi. *A Shattered Usage.*

TEN COMMANDMENTS OF APOLOGETICS

THE GOSPEL FIRST

The mission of the church and every member is to evangelize the world with the good news of Jesus Christ.

APOLOGETICS SECOND

The purpose of apologetics is to answer the challenges and objections that nonbelievers raise concerning the validity of the Christian faith.

STAY WITH THE ESSENTIALS

We must learn the fundamentals of the Christian faith and communicate with nonbelievers. We must always keep it basic and simple.

REMEMBER YOUR GOAL

The purpose of evangelism and apologetics is to convince the nonbeliever of the truth claims of the Christian faith and lead the nonbeliever to a saving relationship with Jesus Christ (Colossians 1:28).

NEVER GIVE PEOPLE A PROBLEM

Never give them a problem or information that would increase their doubt rather than their faith.

FIND OUT THEIR PROBLEM OR OBJECTIONS TO THE CHRISTIAN FAITH

Listen to the nonbeliever and their problems and concerns as to their objections to the Christian faith. This will determine the approach and strategy to prepare the nonbeliever's heart to receive Christ.

AVOID DISTRACTIONS

Discuss in an atmosphere where there are no crowds, television, phone, or children to distract the nonbeliever's attention from the subject under consideration.

APPLY EVANGELISM STRATEGY

Apply the principles of effective evangelism according to the needs of the individual who is being witnessed.

DO NOT BE INTIMIDATED

Most nonbelievers have never read the Bible.

Appendix 2

PRINCIPLES OF APOLOGETICS

The goal of apologetics is to overcome intellectual obstacles to Christianity so that nonbelievers are willing to consider the Gospel.

The winning of souls is more than presenting a compelling argument for the truth of the gospel.

It is the Holy Spirit who brings about conviction to the nonbelievers mind (John 16:8-9).

The Lost are not only wrong—they also are dead in their sins (Ephesians 2:1ff).

The goals of apologetics are to destroy falsehood, to proclaim the faith, and to defend the truth.

We must listen closely to what our opponents are saying and listen to their objections to the Christian faith.

The nonbelief of the lost is a moral problem, not an intellectual one.

Our commitment is to the truth.

Appendix 3

THE UNIQUENESS OF THE CHRISTIAN MESSAGE

- All religions plainly and simply cannot be true.
- Some beliefs are false and we know them to be false.
- Jesus said in John 14:6 that He was the only way to God.
- There is only one way to God.
- Jesus is who He claimed to be.
- All religions are not the same.
- All religions do not point to God.
- All religions do not say that all religions are the same.
- At the heart of every religion is an uncompromising commitment to a particular way of defining who God is—or is not.
- Anyone who claims that all religions are the same betrays an ignorance of all religions.
- Every religion at its core is exclusive.

- All-inclusive philosophies can come only at the loss of truth.
- No religion denies its core beliefs.

GLOSSARY

EPISTEMOLOGY

Epistemology has to do with how we know anything. It is the study of the nature of knowledge.

REVELATION

Revelation is the disclosure of God's will to man. In the Old Testament, God revealed himself in creation, dreams, theophanies, wind, cloud, fire, donkey, angels, Jesus Christ, apostles, and the Bible. God's final word is found in Old Testament and New Testament Scriptures.

REASON

Reason is sometimes referred to in academic circles as "rationalism," which is a philosophy that stresses reason as the means of determining truth. The mind is given authority over senses. The mind can follow principles of logic that will lead to a clearer understanding and conclusion of what is or is not truth.

WORLD VIEW

A world view is a set of presuppositions and assumptions which we hold about the basic makeup of the world.

BELIEF SYSTEM

A belief system is the same as a world view—a set of presuppositions that governs our lives. It is the foundation to which all decisions are made. It is how one views the world in which we live.

SCIENTIFIC METHOD

The scientific method is the belief that science is the only method for discovering truth. Science denies the reality of the supernatural. Science deals only with observable events that are seen in the natural world by the natural eye.

NATURALISM

Naturalism is the philosophical belief system which teaches there is no supernatural realm or intervention into the world—only what nature has given to us.

EMPIRICAL

Empiricism is the belief that reality can be experienced only through our natural physical senses of hearing, seeing, tasting, touching, and smelling. That is how humans communicate in the natural world.

MYSTICISM

Mysticism is a belief that encourages the use of intuition and emotions.

SKEPTICISM

Skepticism is the philosophical belief system which teaches that we cannot really know truth.

AGNOSTICISM

Agnosticism is the belief system that we cannot know what really is the truth. It is a system which suspends judgment because there is not enough sufficient evidence to believe or disbelieve.

ATHEISM

Atheism is the belief that God does not exist.

OTHER BOOKS BY DR. KENNETH GILMORE

*Leadership In African American
Churches of Christ*

The New Covenant: Your Rights and Privileges

What Is Biblical Faith?

The Battle for the Mind

Bring Me The Book

The Apostle's Doctrine

Money: God's Financial Plan For Your Life

Unmasking Satanic Lies

The Authority of The Believer

Principle Centered Living

The Power of The Tongue

Prayer, The Key To Success

God's Spiritual Laws

What Kind of Man Are You

How To Have Success With God
The Decision Is In Your Hand
Bring Me the Book
The Authority of the Believer

TAPE SERIES BY DR. KENNETH GILMORE

New Covenant: Your Rights	2 Tapes
What Is Biblical Faith?	2 Tapes
How To Have Success With God	5 Tapes
Money: God's Financial Plan	2 Tapes
Unmasking Satanic Lies	2 Tapes
The Authority of The Believer	4 Tapes
The Power of The Tongue	3 Tapes
God's Spiritual Laws	6 Tapes
What Kind of Man Are You?	3 Tapes
Principle Centered Living	3 Tapes
The New Testament Church, Which One Is True?	2 Tapes
The Battle For The Mind	4 Tapes
Prayer	4 Tapes

BECOME A COVENANT TRUTH PARTNER WITH KENNETH GILMORE MINISTRIES!

Because of the power that comes through fellowship, commitment and partnership, we invite you to join with Dr. Kenneth Gilmore in fulfilling the vision God has given him. Dr. Gilmore has been given a mandate to teach the Word of God in simple terms so that all can understand.

It's easy to become a Covenant Truth Partner. Simply fill out the form on page 101 and mail it to:

Kenneth Gilmore Ministries
150 S.E. 74th Street
Gainesville, Florida 32641

phone: 352-376-8843
email: Kgmin@bellsouth .net

Our prayer for you is that as you enter covenant with us, God's blessings and manifold riches will be unleashed in your life.

Covenant Truth Partners have sought the Lord and received His confirmation of the worth of this ministry. Therefore, Partners are more than friends, they are loyal, trusted allies in the ministry. We value all of our Covenant Truth Partners and hold them up to God in prayer, minister to them with a personal monthly letter and offer from time to time discounted products for spiritual edification and growth.

THERE IS VALUE IN COVENANT TRUTH PARTNERSHIP!

Yes. I'd like to become a Covenant Truth Partner in prayer and financial support with Kenneth Gilmore Ministries.

_____

Last Name

_____

First Name   Middle Initial

_____

Street Address   Apartment #

_____

City   State   Zip

You can count on me for a monthly pledge of:

❑ $1,000   ❑ $500   ❑ $100

❑ $50   ❑ $25   ❑ $_____

❑ One time gift of $_____

Printed in the United States
17022LVS00002B/9-68